WORD 2000
Expert

Copyright - Editions ENI - March 2000
ISBN: 2-7460-0889-0
Original edition: 2-7460-0906-4

Editions ENI

BP 32125
44021 NANTES Cedex 1

Tél. 02.51.80.15.15
Fax 02.51.80.15.16

e-mail : editions@ediENI.COM
http://www.editions-eni.com

Collection directed by Corinne HERVO

MOUS
Word 2000 Expert

INTRODUCTION 3

DOCUMENT CONTENTS

1.1 Text 11

1.2 Tables 23

1.3 Charts... 47

1.4 Objects.. 61

DOCUMENT PRESENTATION

2.1 Formatting paragraphs/pages 73

2.2 Styles and templates 89

LONG DOCUMENTS

3.1 Notes and bookmarks 109

3.2 Outlines and tables.. 123

3.3 Master documents 139

MAIL MERGE

4.1 Forms...147

4.2 Mail Merge 159

ADVANCED FUNCTIONS

5.1 Macros...183

5.2 Toolbars...193

5.3 Workgroups 201

SUMMARY EXERCISES.....................................223

TABLE OF OBJECTIVES 233

INDEX..237

This book is the ideal tool for an effective preparation of the Word 2000 Expert exam. The MOUS logo on the cover guarantees that this edition has been approved by Microsoft®. It contains the theoretical information corresponding to all the exams themes and you can test your knowledge by working through the practice exercises. If you succeed in completing these exercises without any difficulty, you are ready to take your exam. At the end of the book, you can see a list of the Word 2000 Expert exam objectives, and the number of the lesson and exercise that refer to each of these objectives.

What is the MOUS certification?

The MOUS (Microsoft Office User Specialist) exam gives you the opportunity to obtain a meaningful certification, recognised by Microsoft®, for the Office applications: Word, Excel, Access, PowerPoint, and Outlook. This certification guarantees your level of skill in working with these applications. It can provide a boost to your career ambitions, as it proves that you can use effectively all the features of the Microsoft Office applications and thus offer a high productivity level to your employer. In addition, it would be a certain plus when job-seeking: more and more companies require employment candidates to be MOUS certificate holders.

What are the applications concerned?

You can gain MOUS certification in Office 97 applications (Word, Excel, PowerPoint and Access) and in Office 2000 applications (Word, Excel, PowerPoint, Access and Outlook). MOUS exams also exist for Word 7 and Excel 7. Two exam levels are offered for Word 97, Word 2000, Excel 97 and Excel 2000: a Core level (proficiency) and a second Expert level. For PowerPoint 97 and Access 97, only the Expert certification is available. For PowerPoint 2000, Access 2000 and Outlook 2000, only one level of certification is available.

If you obtain the Expert level for Word 97, Excel 97, PowerPoint 97 and Access 97, you are certified as a Master in Office 97. If you obtain the Expert level for Word 2000 and Excel 2000 as well as MOUS certification in PowerPoint 2000, Access 2000 and Outlook 2000, you are certified as a Master in Office 2000.

How do you apply to sit the exams?

To enrol for the exams, you should contact one of the Microsoft Authorized Testing Centers (or ATC). A list of these centres is available online at this address: http://www.mous.net. Make sure you know for which version of the Office application you wish to obtain the certificate (is it the 97 or 2000 version?).

There is an enrolment fee for each exam.

On the day of the exam, you should carry some form of identification and, if you have already sat a MOUS exam, your ID number.

What happens during the MOUS exam ?

During the exam, you will have a computer that you must use to perform a certain number of tasks on the software in question. Each action you perform to carry out these tasks will be tested in order to make sure that you have done correctly what was asked of you. There are no multiple-choice questions and the exam is not a simulation; you work directly in the application (Word, Excel...).

You are allowed no notes, books, pencils or calculators during the exam. You can consult the application help, but you should be careful not to exceed the exam's time limit.

Each exam is timed; it lasts in general between 45 minutes and one hour.

How do you pass the exam ?

You must carry out a certain percentage of the required tasks correctly, within the allocated time. This percentage varies depending on the exam.

You will be told your result as soon as you have finished your exam. These results are confidential (the data are coded) and are only made known to the candidate and to Microsoft.

What happens then ?

You will receive a Microsoft-approved exam certificate, proving that you hold the specified MOUS (Microsoft Office User Specialist) level.

How this book works

This book is the ideal companion to an effective preparation of the **MOUS Word 2000 Expert** exam. It is divided into several sections, each containing one or more **chapters**. Each section deals with a specific topic: document contents (text, tables, charts, objects), document presentation (formatting paragraphs and pages, outlines, tables of contents, indexes, master documents), forms, mail merge, macros, managing toolbars and workgroups (managing several versions of a document, tracking changes). Each chapter is independent from the others. You can work according to your needs: if you already know how to format paragraphs, for example, you can skip this lesson and go straight to the practice exercise for that chapter, then if you feel you need some extra theory, you can look back at the relevant points in the lesson. You can also study the lesson and/or work through the exercises in any order you wish.

At the end of the book, there is an **index** to help you find the explanations for any action, whenever you need them.

From theory...

Each chapter starts with a **lesson** on the theme in question and the lesson is made up of a variable amount of numbered topics. The lesson should supply you with all the theoretical information necessary to acquire that particular skill. Example screens to illustrate the point discussed enhance the lesson and you will also find tips, tricks and remarks to complement the explanations provided.

...To practice

Test your knowledge by working through the **practice exercise** at the end of each chapter: each numbered heading corresponds to an exercise question. A solution to the exercise follows. These exercises are done using the documents on the CD-ROM accompanying the book, that you install on your own computer (to see how, refer to the INSTALLING THE CD-ROM instructions). In addition to the chapter exercises, seven **summary exercises** dealing with each of the section themes are included at the end of the book. The solutions to these exercises appear as documents on the CD-ROM.

All you need to succeed!

When you can complete all the practice exercises without any hesitation or problems, you are ready to sit the MOUS exam. In the table of contents for each chapter, the topics corresponding to a specific exam objective are marked with this symbol: ▦. At the back of the book, you can also see **the official list of the Word 2000 Expert exam objectives** and for each of these objectives the corresponding lesson and exercise number.

INTRODUCTION
How this book works

The layout of this book

This book is laid out in a specific way with special typefaces and symbols so you can find all the information you need quickly and easily:

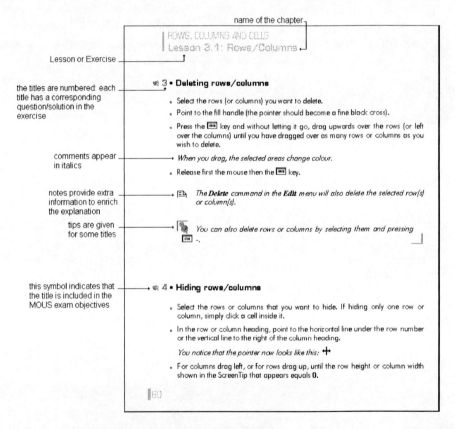

name of the chapter

ROWS, COLUMNS AND CELLS
Lesson 3.1: Rows/Columns

Lesson or Exercise

the titles are numbered: each title has a corresponding question/solution in the exercise

3 ▪ Deleting rows/columns

▫ Select the rows (or columns) you want to delete.
▫ Point to the fill handle (the pointer should become a fine black cross).
▫ Press the [■] key and without letting it go, drag upwards over the rows (or left over the columns) until you have dragged over as many rows or columns as you wish to delete.

comments appear in italics

When you drag, the selected areas change colour.

▫ Release first the mouse then the [■] key.

notes provide extra information to enrich the explanation

*The **Delete** command in the **Edit** menu will also delete the selected row(s) or column(s).*

tips are given for some titles

You can also delete rows or columns by selecting them and pressing [■] -.

this symbol indicates that the title is included in the MOUS exam objectives

4 ▪ Hiding rows/columns

▫ Select the rows or columns that you want to hide. If hiding only one row or column, simply click a cell inside it.
▫ In the row or column heading, point to the horizontal line under the row number or the vertical line to the right of the column heading.

You notice that the pointer now looks like this: ✛

▫ For columns drag left, or for rows drag up, until the row height or column width shown in the ScreenTip that appears equals **0**.

You can distinguish whether an action should be performed with the mouse, the keyboard or with the menu options by referring to the symbol that introduces each action: 🖱, 🎲 and 📋.

Installing the CD-ROM

The CD-ROM provided contains the documents used to work through the practice exercises and the summary exercise solutions. When you follow the installation procedure set out below, a folder called MOUS Word 2000 Expert is created on your hard disk and the CD-ROM documents are decompressed and copied into the created folder. The CD-ROM also contains templates which you should copy into the Word Templates folder.

* Put the CD-ROM into the CD-ROM drive of your computer.

* Start the Windows Explorer: click the **Start** button, point to the **Programs** option then click **Windows Explorer**.

* In the left pane of the Explorer window, scroll through the list until the CD-ROM drive icon appears. Click this icon.

The contents of the CD-ROM appear in the right pane of the Explorer window. The documents you are going to be working on in the exercises appear in their compressed form MOUS Word 2000 Expert.exe, but you can also find them in the Summary and Practice Exercises folders. The templates are in the MOUS Templates folder.

* Double-click the icon of the **MOUS Word 2000 Expert** folder in the right pane of the Explorer window.

*The **MOUS Word 2000 Expert** dialog box appears.*

* Click **Next.**

The installation application offers to create a folder called MOUS Word 2000 Expert.

* Modify the proposed folder name if you wish then click **Next**. If several people are going to be doing the practice exercises on the same computer, you should modify the folder name so each person is working on their own copy of the folder.

■ Click **Yes** to confirm creating the **MOUS Word 2000 Expert** folder.

The installation application decompresses the documents then copies them into the created folder.

■ Click **Finish** when the copying process is finished.

You must now copy the templates into the templates folder used by Word. The default file path used is C:\Windows\Application Data\Microsoft\Templates.

■ Click the folder called **MOUS Templates** that you can see in the right pane of the Explorer window.

■ Open the **Edit** menu then click the **Copy** option to copy the folder into the Windows clipboard.

■ If necessary, scroll through the contents of the left pane of the window until you can see the **Windows** folder; click the plus (+) sign to the left of **Windows** in order to see a list of the folders it contains.

The + sign becomes a - sign.

■ Click the + sign to the left of the **Application Data** folder then click the + sign to the left of the **Microsoft** folder then finally click the **Templates** folder.

By default, the templates are stored in this folder.

■ Use the **Edit - Paste** command to copy the contents of the clipboard into the **Templates** folder.

A dialog box appears while the copy is pasted in.

■ When the copy is finished, click the ☒ button on the **Explorer** window to close it.

You can now put away the CD-ROM and start working on your MOUS exam preparation.

DOCUMENT CONTENTS
Lesson 1.1: Text

1. Sorting paragraphs 12

2. Finding/replacing formatting 13

3. Finding/replacing special characters 14

4. Creating an AutoText entry 15

5. Using an AutoText entry 17

6. Managing existing AutoText entries 19

Practice Exercise 1.1 20

1 ▪ Sorting paragraphs

▪ Select the paragraphs you want to sort.

▪ **Table - Sort**

▪ In the first list in the **Sort by** frame, leave the **Paragraphs** option active to sort by the first word of each paragraph.

If the first words in the selected paragraphs are identical, Word will sort by the second word...

▪ In the **Type** drop-down list, choose the kind of data you want to sort: **Text**, **Number** or **Date** (provided that the at least the day and month or the month and data includes year).

▪ Indicate whether you want to sort in **Ascending** or **Descending** order.

▪ If the first paragraph contains headers and is not to be sorted, activate the **Header row** option in the **My list has** frame.

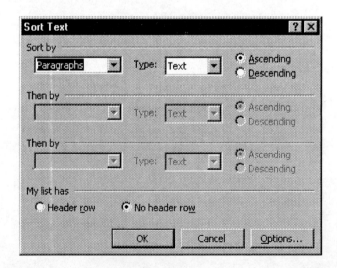

▪ Click **OK**.

▥2 ▪ Finding/replacing formatting

⋇ Place the insertion point where Word is to start searching or select the text concerned by the search or replacement.

⋇ **Edit - Find** or **Replace** or ⌷Ctrl⌷ **F** or ⌷Ctrl⌷ **H**

⋇ If necessary, delete all previous find and replace criteria.

⋇ If you need to, click the **More** button.

*The **No Formatting** button can be used to clear previous find and replace criteria based on formatting.*

⋇ Activate the find and replace criteria using the **Format** button.

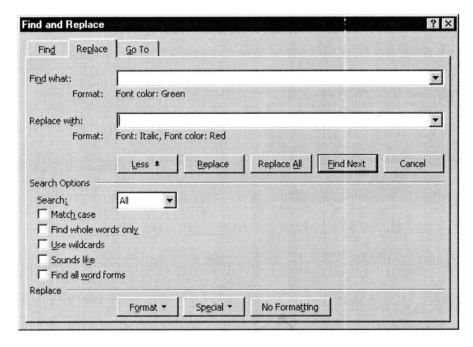

Text that is coloured green will be changed to red and put in italics.

▪ If the replacements are to be made one-by-one, click the **Find Next** button, then the **Replace** button. To replace all the text at once, click **Replace All**.

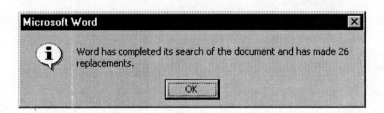

▪ Click **OK** when all the replacements have been made, then choose to **Close** the dialog box.

If you have selected text, Word will ask you if you want to continue searching the rest of the document.

▪ Click **No** then **Close**.

▣3 ▪ Finding/replacing special characters

▪ Place the insertion point where Word is to start searching or select the text concerned.

▪ **Edit - Find** or **Replace** or ⌨Ctrl **F** or ⌨Ctrl **H**

▪ Set your criteria as you would for any search (or replacement), but use the **Special** button to choose the special character in question.

The character is shown as a code.

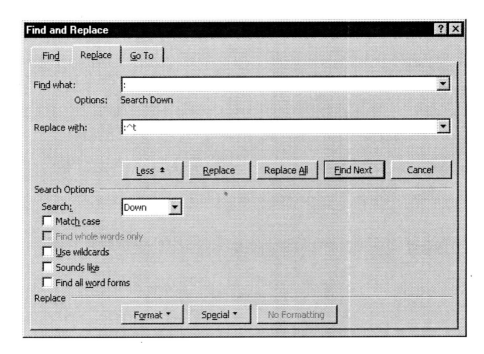

The code for a tab character is ^t.

⬚ Choose to **Replace All** or make replacements one-by-one using the **Find Next** button.

⬚ When you have finished, click **OK** then **Close**.

If you have selected text, Word asks you if you want to continue searching the rest of the document.

⬚ Click **No** then **Close**.

4 ▪ Creating an AutoText entry

An AutoText entry allows you to save text that you use often, along with its formatting (such as addresses, signatures...).

⬚ If the AutoText is for all documents, open a document based on the Normal.dot template, or the personal template on which you usually base your documents.

If the AutoText concerns only a certain type of document, based on a particular template, open a document based on this template.

* Enter the contents of the AutoText, remembering to format the text as necessary.

* Select the AutoText contents.

* **Insert - AutoText - AutoText** or

  The tool can be found on the *AutoText* toolbar.

* In the **Look in** list, choose the name of the template that is to contain the AutoText.

* Give the name of the AutoText in the **Enter AutoText entries here** box.

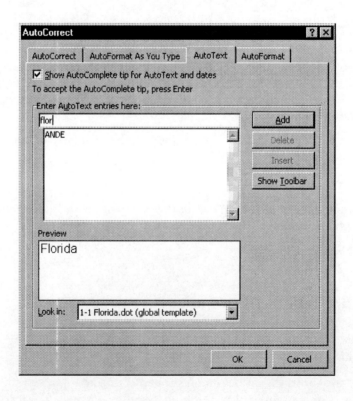

※ Click **Add**.

📑 *The AutoText entries will be created when the corresponding template is saved: if they have been added to a template other than **Normal.dot**, Word asks you if you want to save the template when you close the document. If the AutoText entries have been made in **Normal.dot**, you will be asked to save the changes when you close Word.*

*Once you have specified where AutoText entries are to be saved, you can use the **Insert - AutoText - New** menu or ⌐Alt⌐F3⌐ or click the **New** button on the **AutoText** toolbar to create new AutoText entries.*

5 ▪ Using an AutoText entry

※ Place the insertion point where you want to insert the AutoText.

※ **Insert - AutoText - AutoText** or

※ In the **Look in** list, activate the appropriate template.

※ Select the AutoText you want to insert.

※ Click **Insert**.

*When the template is chosen in the **Look in** list, the AutoText entries linked to the active style are listed at the bottom of the **AutoText** menu or on the second button on the **AutoText** toolbar. You can also insert an AutoText by clicking it.*

DOCUMENT CONTENTS
Lesson 1.1: Text

❖ First method

- Place the insertion point where you want to insert the AutoText.

- Start to type the name of the AutoText.

1513:	the Spaniard *Juan Ponce de León* discovers Florida. The state was at that time populated by Seminoles. The peninsula was navigated in 1528 by Pánfilo de Narvárez and in 1539 by Hernando de Soto.
1562 - 1565:	Florida is colonised by a group of French Huguenots under the command of *Jean Ribaut*.
1565:	Florida is conquered by the Spanish, under the command of *Pedro Menedez de Avliés*. The French establishments are destroyed and Jean Ribaut is executed. Menedez founds Saint Augustine, the oldest town in the United States.
1738:	Spain regains flor after the American War of Independence.
1763:	Spain cedes Florida to England following the Seven Years war.

The AutoComplete feature is set in action and Word offers to finish the rest of the AutoText.

- Confirm by pressing ↵.

*This semi-automatic completion is only available if the **Show AutoComplete tip for AutoText and dates** option is active in the **AutoCorrect** dialog box (**Tools - AutoCorrect - AutoText** tab).*

Second method

- Place the insertion point where you want to insert the AutoText.

- Type the name of the AutoText entry you want to use.

- Press F3.

6 ▪ Managing existing AutoText entries

Deleting an AutoText entry

▪ **Insert - AutoText - AutoText** or

▪ If necessary, choose the template that contains the entry in the **Look in** list.

▪ Click the name of the AutoText you want to delete.

▪ Click the **Delete** button.

The entry disappears from the list immediately.

▪ Close the dialog box.

Changing the contents of an AutoText entry

▪ If necessary, insert the AutoText and make your changes.

▪ Select the AutoText contents.

▪ **Insert - AutoText - AutoText** or

▪ Click the entry's original name.

▪ Click the **Add** button.

▪ Confirm that you want to redefine the entry by clicking **Yes**.

📄 *Changing or deleting an AutoText entry will change the template in which it is saved.*

🔎 *To print a list of the AutoText entries in a given template, open a document based on the template and run* ***File - Print***. *Select* ***AutoText entries*** *in the* ***Print what*** *list and click* ***OK***.

DOCUMENT CONTENTS
Exercise 1.1: Text

Below, you can see **Practice Exercise** 1.1. This exercise is made up of 6 steps. If you do not know how to complete one of the steps, go back to the lesson to refer to the corresponding title. When you have finished, check your work by reading the **Solution** on the next page.

Steps that are likely to be tested on the exam are marked with a ⊞ symbol. It is however recommended that you follow the whole exercise in order to gain a complete understanding of the lesson.

☞ **Practice Exercise 1.1**

To complete exercise 1.1, you will need to open *1-1 Florida Intro* in the *MOUS Word 2000 Expert* folder.

⊞ 1. Sort the paragraphs in the section about the **History** of Florida.

⊞ 2. Replace all the text in **Green** with text in **Red** and in **Italic** throughout the whole document.

⊞ 3. In the **History** of Florida section, replace all the colons (:) followed by a space with a colon followed by a tab.

4. Create an AutoText entry called **flor** using one the words "Florida", with the text in blue.

5. Insert this AutoText entry using **flor** after **1738 Spain regains**.

6. Delete the AutoText entry called **ANDE**, which was previously inserted into the **1-1 Florida.dot** template then close the document, saving the changes and those made to the **1-1 Florida.dot** template.

If you want to put what you have learned into practice in a real document, you can work on the summary exercise 1 for the DOCUMENT CONTENTS section that you can find at the end of this book.

It is often possible to perform a task in several different ways, but here only the quickest solution is presented. Go back to the lesson to see the other techniques that can be used.

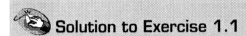

Solution to Exercise 1.1

1. To sort the paragraphs in the section about the History of Florida, select the text from the paragraph that starts **1763** to the paragraph that starts **1868**.
   Use **Table - Sort**.
   In the first list in the **Sort by** frame, leave the **Paragraphs** option selected.
   In the **Type** drop-down list, leave the **Text** option active and make sure the sort is in **Ascending** order.
   Leave the **No header row** option selected.
   Click **OK**.

2. To replace all the text in green by text in red and italics, press ⌨Ctrl ⌨⌐ to return to the beginning of the document.
   Activate **Edit - Replace**.
   If necessary, clear the previous find and replace criteria.
   Click the **More** button if you need to.
   Leave the insertion point in the **Find what** box, click the **Format** button and activate the **Font** option. In the **Font color** list, choose the **Green** then click **OK**.
   Click in the **Replace with** box, open the list on the **Format** button and choose **Font**. In the **Font color** list, choose the **Red** and in the **Font style** box, click **Italic**. Click **OK**.
   Click the **Replace All** button.
   When all the replacements have been made, click **OK** then **Close**.

3. To replace the colons (:) followed by a space with a colon followed by a tab in the History section, select the text from **1513...** to **1868...**.
Run **Edit - Replace**.
Click the **More** button if you need to.
In the **Find what** box, type: followed by ⎵Space⎵ then click the **No Formatting** button.
Click in the **Replace with** box and click the **No Formatting** button again to remove the formatting from the previous find and replace.
Enter the colon character, click the **Special** button and choose the **Tab Character** option.
Click **Replace All**, then **No** when Word asks if you want to search the rest of the document.
Click **Close** to close the **Find and Replace** dialog box.

4. To create an AutoText entry called **flor**, select the word **Florida** (which is in blue) in the **1513...** paragraph.
Use **Insert - AutoText - AutoText**.
In the **Look in** list, choose **1-1 Florida.dot**, the template on which **1-1 Florida Intro** is based.
Select the contents of the **Enter AutoText entries here** box and type **flor**.
Click **Add**.

5. To insert the "flor" AutoText entry after "1783 Spain regains", place the insertion point after the space that follows the word **regains**.
Type **flor** then press ⏎.

6. To delete the "ANDE" AutoText entry, use **Insert - AutoText - AutoText**.
In the **Look in** list, choose **1-1 Florida.dot**.
In the **Enter AutoText entries here** box, click the name **ANDE** then click **Delete**.
Click **Close**.

To close the document and save the changes you have made, and the changes to the template, use **File - Close** then click **Yes** twice.

DOCUMENT CONTENTS
Lesson 1.2: Tables

1. Sorting a list or table... 24

2. Adding up a column/row 27

3. Managing a table as in a spreadsheet... 28

4. Showing/hiding field codes 31

5. Updating a field 31

6. Embedding a Microsoft Excel worksheet
   into a Microsoft Word document... 32

7. Copying Microsoft Excel data into Microsoft Word by linking 36

8. Editing a Microsoft Excel worksheet inserted
   in a Microsoft Word document... 37

Practice Exercise 1.2 40

1 ▪ Sorting a list or table

Sorting a list

A list is composed of a series of paragraphs that contain text presented in columns (called fields), separated by tab stops or semi-colons. Example:

SURNAME	→	NAME	→	DEPARTMENT	→	EXTENSION¶
WALKER	→	Tim	→	Accounts		1012¶
EVANS	→	Rachel	→	Sales	→	1013¶
MITCHELL	→	Sarah	→	Production	→	1562¶
ANDERSON	→	Mark	→	Sales	→	1133¶
BROWN	→	Kathleen	→	Sales	→	1141¶
PARKER	→	Andrea	→	Accounts	→	1419¶
BUTCHER	→	Tom	→	Production	→	1010¶
LOXTON	→	Steve	→	Purchasing	→	1942¶
WATT	→	Chris	→	Sales	→	1420¶
JULIANO	→	Lucia	→	Production	→	1949¶
HUTCHISON	→	Irene	→	Accounts	→	1401¶
LANGLEY	→	Paul	→	Accounts	→	1500¶
ANDREWS	→	Robin	→	Purchasing	→	1177¶
LEWIS	→	Alison	→	Sales	→	1502¶
BYRNE	→	Philip	→	Production	→	1017¶
OTTERMAN	→	Dan	→	Sales	→	1120¶
MORGAN	→	Sian	→	Sales	→	0811¶

▪ Select the list of paragraphs you want to sort.

▪ **Table - Sort**

Notice that you can sort according to three different criteria.

▪ If the first paragraph in the selection contains headers and is not to be sorted, activate the **Header row** option in the **My list has** frame.

▪ In the first list in the **Sort by** frame, choose the field number or header by which you wish to sort.

▪ In the **Type** list, choose the kind of data you want to sort: **Text**, **Number** or **Date** (for data composed of at least a day and month, or month and year).

* Indicate whether you want to sort in **Ascending** or **Descending** order.

* If, in the column by which you are sorting, several rows contain the same data, define a second set of criteria in the first **Then by** frame, following the same principles.

* Define a third set of criteria in the second **Then by** frame if you need to.

* Click **OK** to sort.

 *You can change the field separators by going to the **Sort Options** dialog box (**Table - Sort, Options** button) and using the options in the **Separate fields at** frame.*

Sorting a table

* In the table, select the items you want to sort. If you want to sort the whole table, you do not need to select it, just click inside it.

* **Table - Sort**

* If the first paragraph in the selection contains headers and is not to be sorted, activate the **Header row** option in the **My list has** frame.

* In the first list in the **Sort by** frame, select the column header by which you want to sort.

* If necessary, choose a **Type** in the second list.

* Indicate whether you want to sort in **Ascending** or **Descending** order.

DOCUMENT CONTENTS
Lesson 1.2: Tables

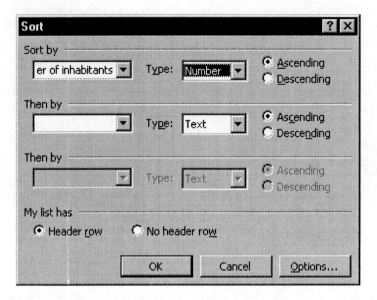

* If several of the cells in the column by which you are sorting contain the same data, use the same principles to define the second column to sort by in the first **Then by** frame.

* If necessary, set criteria in the second **Then by** frame.

* Once you have defined all your criteria, click **OK**.

If your sort is not successful, use the button to restore the initial order.

You can also use the or tools on the **Tables and Borders** toolbar to sort the contents of the active column in ascending or descending order.

Sorting a single column in a table

※ Select the column you want to sort.

※ **Table - Sort**

※ Keep **Column** as the choice in the first **Sort by** list.

※ Indicate the **Type** of the column contents.

※ Click the **Options** button.

※ Activate the **Sort column only** choice in the **Sort options** frame.

※ Click **OK** twice.

▣2 ▪ Adding up a column/row

※ If necessary, show the **Tables and Borders** toolbar.

※ Click the cell in which you want the result to appear.

※ Click the Σ tool.

➤ Recommended route for tour of main tourist attractions:

Start	Arrive	Distance in miles
Miami	Key West	155
Key West	Naples	220
Naples	Sarasota	105
Sarasota	Orlando	140
Orlando	Cape Canaveral	60
Cape Canaveral	Miami	220
Distance travelled	in miles	900
	in kilometres (1 mile = 1.609 km)	

By default, Word adds up the cells above.

🕮3 ▪ Managing a table as in a spreadsheet

The basic principles

▪ Each column is identified by a letter (the first column is A, the second column is B...) and each row is identified by a number (the first row is 1, the second row is 2...).
The reference of a cell is defined by associating the column letter and the row number (A2, B5...).

▪ To list adjacent cells, give the reference of the first cell, type a colon (:) and the reference of the last cell (e.g. C2:C4).
To list non-adjacent cells, use a semi-colon as a separator (e.g. B5;D5).

Entering a calculation formula

▪ Activate the result cell.

▪ **Table - Formula**

▪ In the **Formula** box, enter your formula after the = sign, using the cell references and the following mathematical operators:

- to subtract,

/ to divide,

* to multiply,

% to calculate a percentage,

^ to calculate to the power of,

+ to add.

▪ Choose a **Number format** if necessary.

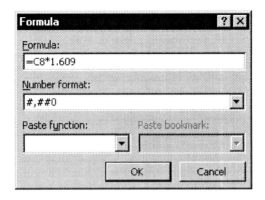

▪ Click **OK**.

Using a calculation function in a table

▪ Activate the result cell.

▪ **Table - Formula**

▪ If necessary, delete the contents of the **Formula** box, except for the = sign.

▪ In the **Paste function** list, choose the function that corresponds to the calculation you want to make.

▪ In the **Formula** box, indicate the items concerned by the formula by inserting, between brackets, the following:

ABOVE	all the cells above.
BELOW	all the cells below.
LEFT	all the cells to the left.
RIGHT	all the cells to the right.
Cell ref.:Cell ref.	adjacent cells.
Cell ref.;Cell ref.	non-adjacent cells.

▪ Choose the **Number format** to be applied to the result.

▪ Click **OK**.

Formatting a calculation result

■ Create your calculation formula.

■ Open the **Number format** list and choose a format (the effect of the different formats is shown below using the number -3637.54):

#,##0	- 3,638
#,##0.00	-3,637.54
£#,##0.00;(£#,##0.00)	(£3,637.54)
$#,##0.00 ;($#,##0.00)	($3,637.54)
0	-3638
0%	-3638%
0.00	-3637.54
0.00%	-3637.54%

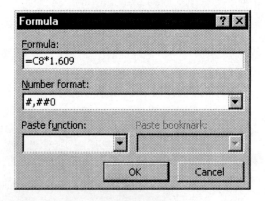

■ Click **OK** to insert the formula in the table.

📄 *Calculation results are in fact **FIELD** results.*
Values are shown if you are in results view and not field codes view.

4 ▪ Showing/hiding field codes

* If you want to show/hide a field code, place the insertion point on the field and press [Shift][F9].

* If you want to show/hide the field codes throughout the document, press [Alt][F9].

Start	Arrive	Distance in miles
Miami	Key West	155
Key West	Naples	220
Naples	Sarasota	105
Sarasota	Orlando	140
Orlando	Cap Canaveral	60
Cap Canaveral	Miami	220
Distance travelled	in miles	{ =SUM(ABOVE) }
	in kilometres (1 mile = 1.609 km)	{ =C8*1.609 \# "# ##0" }

The formulas appear between braces. Word saves the formulas and not the values, which means that if a value is changed, the result can be updated.

5 ▪ Updating a field

* Place the insertion point in the field you want to update.

* Press [F9].

   *You can also right-click the field to be updated and choose **Update Field**.*

▣6 ▪ Embedding a Microsoft Excel worksheet into a Microsoft Word document

This feature allows you to create an object in Word that contains a Microsoft Excel worksheet (existing or new).

Embedding a new sheet

This method involves opening Excel (without leaving Word) in order to create a table.

▪ Place the insertion point where you want to insert the object.

▪ **Insert - Object - Create New** tab

▪ In the **Object type** list, choose **Microsoft Excel Worksheet**.

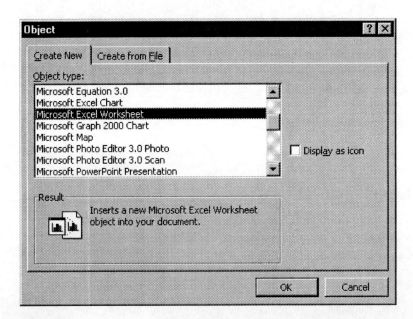

▪ If you want the sheet to be shown as an icon and not as an Excel sheet, activate **Display as icon**.

If you activate this option, Microsoft Excel is opened in a new window; you can save the Excel worksheet you have created.

※ Click **OK**.

The worksheet appears in a frame with a hatched border. The Word menus and toolbars are replaced with those from Excel.

※ Create the object using the features and options in the Excel application.

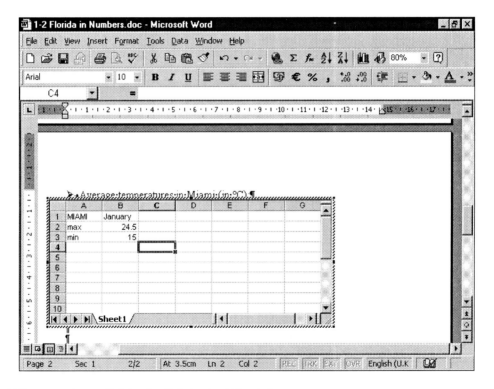

※ When you have finished, click in the Word document.

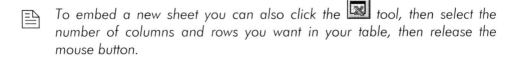

To embed a new sheet you can also click the ▣ tool, then select the number of columns and rows you want in your table, then release the mouse button.

Embedding an existing worksheet

This feature allows you to embed a complete worksheet from an existing workbook.

▪ **Insert - Object**

▪ Click the **Create from File** tab.

▪ Enter the name of the Microsoft Excel workbook that contains the worksheet you want to embed in the **File name** box, or use the **Browse** button to select the workbook.

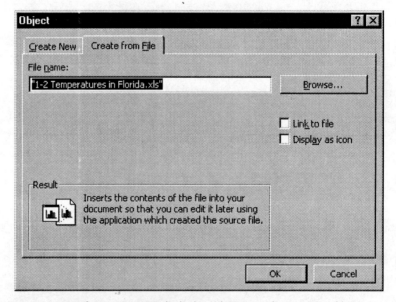

▪ Activate **Link to file** if you want to link the object to the source file.

▪ If appropriate, activate **Display as icon**.

* Click **OK**.

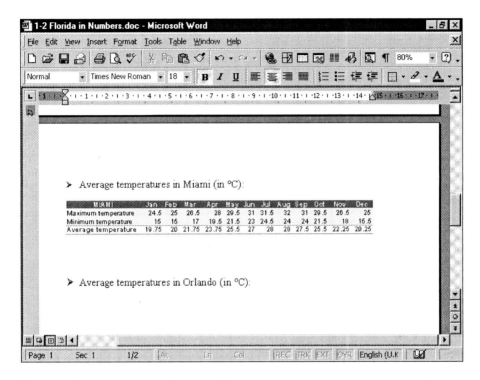

The worksheet appears in the Word document. It is an object that can be managed like any other Word object.

If you have activated the **Display as icon** option in the **Object** dialog box, the sheet appears as:

If the workbook contains several sheets, the sheet embedded into Word is the one that is active when the workbook is opened.

7 ▪ Copying Microsoft Excel data into Microsoft Word by linking

▪ Open the Microsoft Excel application and the workbook that contains the data you want to copy.

▪ Select the Microsoft Excel data that you want to copy (table, chart...).

▪ **Edit - Copy** or 📋 or ⌊Ctrl⌋ **C**

▪ Open Microsoft Word application and the document into which you want to copy the data.

▪ Place the insertion point where the data are to appear.

▪ **Edit - Paste Special**

▪ Activate the **Paste link** option.

▪ Select the format in which the data are to be pasted from the **As** list.

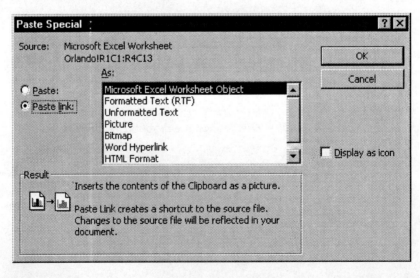

▪ Click **OK**.

The data appear at the insertion point. Any changes made to the Microsoft Excel data will be immediately updated in Microsoft Word as updating is automatic by default.

8 ▪ Editing a Microsoft Excel worksheet inserted in a Microsoft Word document

The way in which you make changes to a worksheet depends on the way in which it was inserted.

Changing a linked worksheet

▪ **Edit - Links**

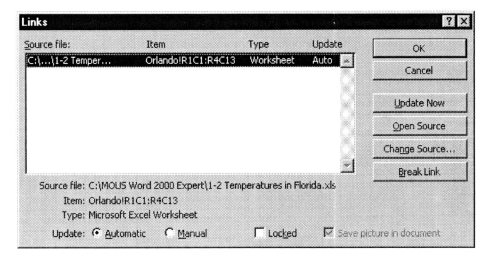

▪ Click the linked object, then the **Open Source** button.

You can also double-click the Microsoft Excel worksheet object.

Microsoft Excel starts and the workbook containing the sheet opens.

▪ Make your changes.

The changes you make are applied to the object in the Word document straight away.

* Close Microsoft Excel using **File - Exit** or click in the source document.

  If you close Excel without saving the workbook, the changes you made are still saved in the Word document. In this case, you need to make a manual update by pressing .

 *Links are, by default, updated automatically if the **Update automatic links at Open** option is active under the **General** tab of the **Options (Tools - Options)** dialog box. To change the type of update, use **Edit - Links** then, having clicked the object in question, choose the **Update** type: **Automatic** or **Manual**. You can update a manual link by pressing* [F9].

Changing an embedded worksheet

* Double-click the embedded object, which represents the worksheet you want to modify, to open it.

  If the object has been embedded as a worksheet, Microsoft Excel menus and toolbars replace those of Word and the worksheet appears in a hatched border. If you embedded the object as an icon, Excel opens and the worksheet is shown in the Excel window.

* Make the required changes to the embedded object.

* If you have been editing an embedded object in Word, click anywhere in the document (outside the object, of course) to return to Word.
  If you have been editing an embedded object in a separate Excel window, return to Word by using **File - Exit** to close Excel.

When you embed a worksheet selected in an existing workbook, the entire workbook is inserted into the document but you can only see one sheet. To see other sheets, double-click the Microsoft Excel object, then click the worksheet you want to see.

To edit a Microsoft Excel object when you do not have Excel installed on your computer, select the object and use ***Edit - Worksheet Object - Convert*** *and choose a file format which is managed by an application you have.*

You can also click the object and use ***Edit - Worksheet Object*** *and choose* ***Open*** *to make changes directly in Microsoft Excel, or choose* ***Edit*** *if you want to remain in Word to make your changes.*

DOCUMENT CONTENTS
Exercise 1.2: Tables

Below, you can see **Practice Exercise** 1.2. This exercise is made up of 8 steps. If you do not know how to complete one of the steps, go back to the lesson to refer to the corresponding title. When you have finished, check your work by reading the **Solution** on the next page.

Steps that are likely to be tested on the exam are marked with a ⊞ symbol. It is however recommended that you follow the whole exercise in order to gain a complete understanding of the lesson.

☞ Practice Exercise 1.2

*In order to complete exercise 1.2, you will need to open **1-2 Florida in Numbers** in the **MOUS Word 2000 Expert** folder.*

⊞ 1. Sort the first table in the document in ascending order by number of inhabitants.

⊞ 2. In the second table in the document, add the distances in miles and display the result in the green cell.

⊞ 3. Remaining in the second table, calculate the total distance in kilometres by converting the total in miles and display the result in the pink cell (1 mile is equal to 1.609 kilometres). Apply a thousands format to the result of this formula.

4. Show the field codes for the entire document.

5. Hide the field codes for the entire document then, in the second table, change the number of miles between **Miami** and **Key West** to **160** miles. Update the formulas in this table.

6. Embed a new Excel worksheet in page 2 of the document, underneath the **Average temperatures in Miami (in °C)** paragraph. Enter the data shown below:

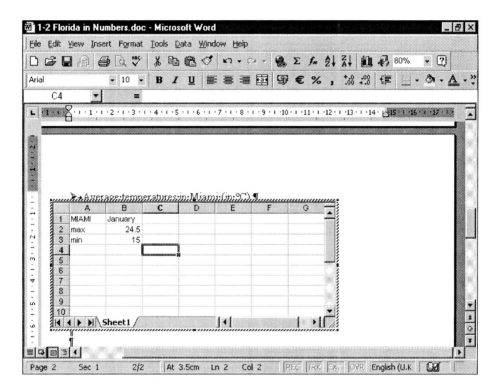

Now undo this insertion and, in its place, embed the active sheet from the **1-2 Temperatures in Florida** worksheet, which can be found in the **MOUS Word 2000 Expert** folder. Insert the object without linking.

DOCUMENT CONTENTS
Exercise 1.2: Tables

▦ 7. Copy, with a link, cells A1 to M4 from the worksheet called **Orlando** in the **1-2 Temperatures in Florida** worksheet (in the **MOUS Word 2000 Expert** folder), pasting this data below the **Average temperatures in Orlando (in °C)** paragraph, at the end of the document. Close Microsoft Excel and return to the **1-2 Florida in Numbers** document.

▦ 8. The maximum January temperature in Orlando is actually 22°C. Change this information, then leave Excel, saving the changes to the workbook. Return to the Word document **1-2 Florida in Numbers**.

If you want to put what you have learned into practice in a real document, you can work on the summary exercise 1 for the DOCUMENT CONTENTS section that you can find at the end of this book.

It is often possible to perform a task in several different ways, but here only the quickest solution is presented. Go back to the lesson to see the other techniques that can be used.

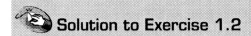

Solution to Exercise 1.2

1. To sort the first table in the document in ascending order by number of inhabitants, click in the table then use **Table - Sort**.
   If necessary, activate the **Header row** option in the **My list has** frame.
   In the first list in the **Sort by** frame, choose the **Number of inhabitants** column header.
   Activate the **Number** option in the **Type** list, then make sure the **Ascending** option is active.
   Click **OK**.

2. To add up the total distance in miles and show the result in the green cell in the second table, first click in this cell.

   If necessary, display the **Tables and Borders** toolbar by clicking the tool.

   Click the Σ tool.

3. To convert the total number of miles to kilometres and insert the result in the pink cell, click in this cell and use **Table - Formula**.
   In the **Formula** box, type = **C8*1.609**
   In the **Number format list**, choose the **#,##0** format.
   Click **OK**.

4. To show all the field codes in the document, press Alt F9.

5. To hide the field codes, press Alt F9 again.

To replace the number of miles between **Miami** and **Key West**, select **155** then type **160**.

To update the calculation formulas in this table, click in the first formula (which displays the result 900) and press F9. Now click in the second formula (showing the result 1488) and press F9 again.

6. To embed a new worksheet in page 2 of this document, below the paragraph "Average temperatures in Miami (in °C)", click in the empty paragraph that follows.
Use the command **Insert - Object**, **Create New** tab.
In the **Object type** list, choose **Microsoft Excel Worksheet** then click **OK**.
Enter the following data:

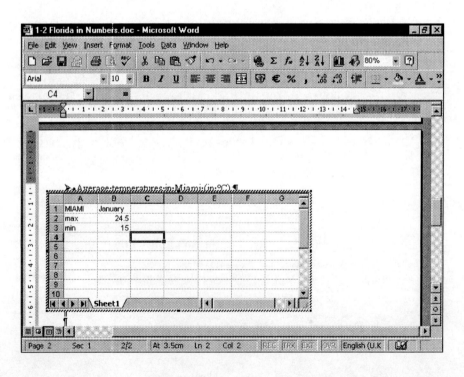

One you have finished, click in the Word document then use **Edit - Undo Object**.

To embed the active worksheet in the "1-2 Temperatures in Florida" workbook, use **Insert - Object**.

Click the **Create from File** tab and then the **Browse** button.

Select the **1-2 Temperatures in Florida** workbook in the **MOUS Word 2000 Expert** folder.

Click the **Insert** button to close the **Browse** dialog box, then **OK** to insert the worksheet.

7. To copy cells A1 to M4 from the "Orlando" worksheet in "1-2 Temperatures in Florida", with a link, at the end of the Word document, start by opening Excel.

Open the **1-2 Temperatures in Florida** workbook in the **MOUS Word 2000 Expert** folder.

Click the **Orlando** tab and select cells **A1** to **M4**.

Click the tool.

On the taskbar, click the button that corresponds to the **1-2 Florida in Numbers** Word document, then press Ctrl End to send the insertion point to the end of the document.

Use **Edit - Paste Special**, then activate the **Paste link** option.

In the **As** list, choose **Microsoft Excel Worksheet Object** then click **OK**.

To close Microsoft Excel, click the **1-2 Temperatures in Florida** button on the taskbar and use **File - Exit**. Return to the **1-2 Florida in Numbers** document by clicking the corresponding button on the taskbar, if necessary.

8. To change the maximum January temperature in Orlando to 22°C, double-click the last table you inserted (which refers to the temperatures in Orlando). Excel opens in a new window.

   Click in cell **B2** in the **Orlando** worksheet, enter **22** and press ↵.

   To close Excel, use **File – Exit**.
   Click **Yes** to save the changes to the workbook.
   Return to **1-2 Florida in Numbers** by clicking the corresponding button on the taskbar, if necessary.

DOCUMENT CONTENTS
Lesson 1.3: Charts

1. Creating a chart 48

2. Importing a Microsoft Excel worksheet into a chart 51

3. Editing a chart 53

Practice Exercise 1.3 57

▦1 ▪ Creating a chart

Starting Microsoft Graph

▪ If the data you want to represent already exist, copy them onto the clipboard.

▪ Place the insertion point where you want to the chart to appear.

▪ **Insert - Object**, and double-click **Microsoft Graph 2000 Chart**.

*After a few seconds, a window called **Datasheet** appears, containing the data represented in the chart that has appeared, surrounded by a hatched border. The data currently in this window are example data.*

The menus and toolbars belong to Microsoft Graph 2000.

▪ It is a good idea to reorganise your screen by moving the **Datasheet** window so that you can see the chart properly.

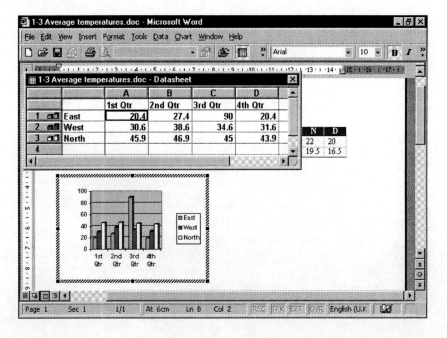

❋ Insert the data you want to represent into the datasheet then define the chart settings (see below).

Clearing the datasheet cells

❋ Select the cells you want to clear.

❋ **Edit - Clear**

❋ Choose whether you want to clear **All**, the **Contents** or the **Formats** of the cells.

The numerical data is no longer shown in the chart, but Microsoft Graph still treats the three rows and four columns as example data.

Entering data in the datasheet

❋ Click in the first cell concerned by the data entry, or the first destination cell of the copy.

❋ Enter the data you want to represent in the chart or insert the contents of the clipboard by **Edit - Paste**.

Data is entered as with a table in Word. Notice that the chart follows the changes you make.

Deleting rows/columns in the datasheet

❋ Select the rows/columns you want to delete by clicking the header of the first and dragging the mouse pointer.

❋ **Edit - Delete** or Ctrl -

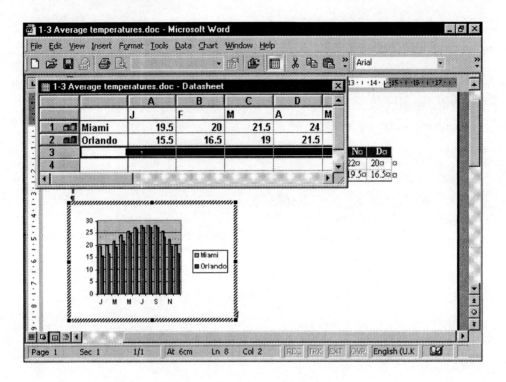

Leaving Microsoft Graph

⁜ Click outside the datasheet or chart, anywhere in the Word document.

📄 *A chart is an object that can be resized, moved... like any other drawing object.*

⊞2 ▪ Importing a Microsoft Excel worksheet into a chart

» In Microsoft Graph, place the insertion point in the datasheet. If you have left Microsoft Graph, double-click the chart object to open it.

» In the datasheet, click in the first destination cell for the imported data.

» **Edit - Import File**

» In the **Look in** list, choose the drive and the folder that contain the workbook you want to import.

The *Files of type* box shows *Microsoft Excel Files*.

» Double-click the name of the Excel workbook you want to import.

» If you have selected an Excel workbook created using version 5.0 or later, select the sheet you want to import.

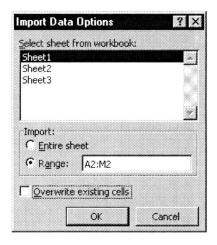

You can only import one sheet.

- To import all the data in the worksheet, click the **Entire sheet** option in the **Import** frame.
  To import only part of the data, click the **Range** option and enter the cell references as follows: **First cell:Last cell**.

- Make sure that the **Overwrite existing cells** option is active if you want to replace all the data in the datasheet with the imported data.

- Click **OK**.

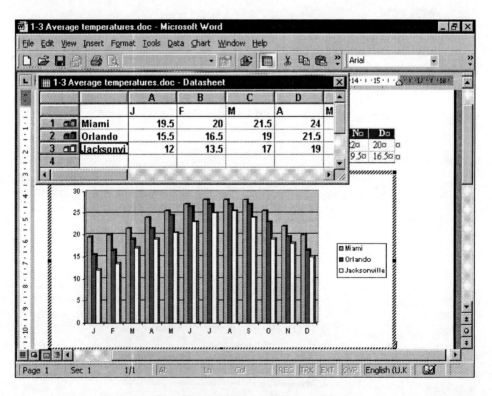

The datasheet and the chart are updated immediately.

You can import up to 4000 rows and 4000 columns of data, but only 255 data series can be shown in the chart.

3 ▪ Editing a chart

Opening Microsoft Graph 2000

▪ Double-click the chart you want to change or select it and use **Edit - Chart Object - Edit**.

▪ Make your changes to the chart or datasheet.

Indicating whether the series are in rows or columns

▪ **Data - Series in Rows** or **Series in Columns**

Changing the chart type

▪ **Chart - Chart Type**

The names of all the main chart types are listed.

▪ Choose the **Chart type** you want to use.

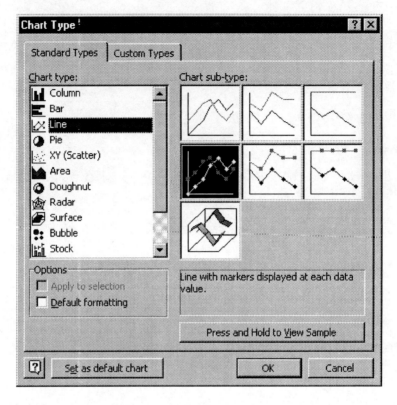

■ Double-click the **Chart sub-type** you want.

Managing the chart legend

■ **Chart - Chart Options**

■ Click the **Legend** tab.

■ Choose to **Show legend** or not.

■ Choose where you want to position the legend.

■ Click **OK**.

Adding a title to the chart/an axis

■ **Chart - Chart Options**

■ Click the **Titles** tab.

■ Enter the title you want to add in the appropriate text box.

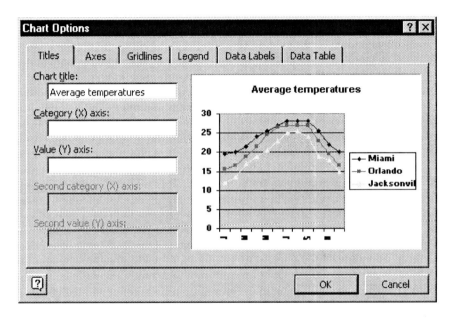

■ Click **OK**.

Changing the formatting of a chart item

■ Click in the item to select it; to select an axis, click one of the labels.

When an item is selected, it is surrounded by handles. Black handles indicate that the item can be moved and/or resized.

■ Open the **Format** menu and activate the first option in this menu, which corresponds to the name of the selected item, or double-click the item you want to change.

■ Activate the tab that corresponds to the feature you want to change.

*The **Format** dialog box displays different tabs according to the selected item.*

■ Make the required formatting changes.

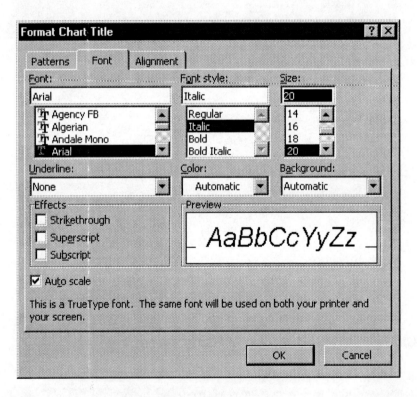

■ Click **OK**.

Below, you can see **Practice Exercise** 1.3. This exercise is made up of 3 steps. If you do not know how to complete one of the steps, go back to the lesson to refer to the corresponding title. When you have finished, check your work by reading the **Solution** on the next page.

All the steps in this exercise are likely to be tested in the exam.

☞ Practice Exercise 1.3

In order to complete exercise 1.3, you will need to open *1-3 Average temperatures.doc* in the *MOUS Word 2000 Expert* folder.

1. Use the data in the table to create a chart like the one shown here:

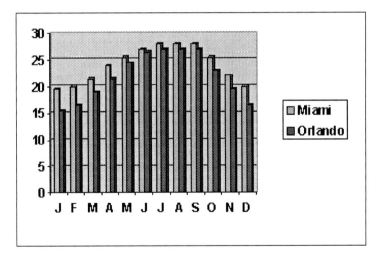

Leave Microsoft Graph, then resize the chart object, keeping its proportions, until it is the same width as the table (about 16cm/4 inches).

DOCUMENT CONTENTS
Exercise 1.3: Charts

▣ 2. In the chart created in the previous step, import the data from cells **A2** to **M2** from the first worksheet in the **1-3 Temperatures in Jacksonville** workbook, which is stored in the **MOUS Word 2000 Expert** folder (the data you are importing are the average temperatures taken in Jacksonville). These data should be added to the third row of the chart datasheet. When you have finished, leave Microsoft Graph.

▣ 3. Make changes to the chart, using the screen below as a guide:

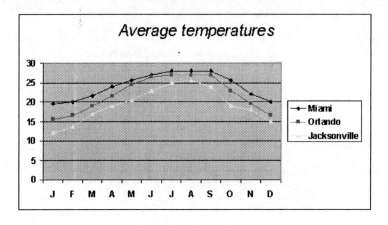

You need to:

- change the chart type: this is a **Line** chart,
- add the title **Average temperatures** to the chart,
- apply an italics format to this title.

When you have finished, leave Microsoft Graph.

If you want to put what you have learned into practice in a real document, you can work on the summary exercise 1 for the DOCUMENT CONTENTS section that you can find at the end of this book.

It is often possible to perform a task in several different ways, but here only the quickest solution is presented. Go back to the lesson to see the other techniques that can be used.

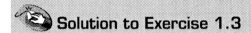
Solution to Exercise 1.3

1. To create a chart, using the data in the table, that looks like the one shown in step 1 of the exercise, click inside the table then use **Table - Select - Table**. Click the ⧉ tool to copy the data to the clipboard.

Press Ctrl End to send the insertion point to the end of the document.

Run **Insert - Object** and double-click the **Microsoft Graph 2000 Chart** option.

By dragging, select the cells from the first cell in the datasheet to cell **D3**. Use **Edit - Clear - All**.

Next, click in the first cell then paste the data from the clipboard using **Edit - Paste**.

In order to delete the row called **3-D column**, which serves no purpose, click the header and use **Edit - Delete**.

To leave Microsoft Graph, click outside of the chart or the datasheet, anywhere in the **1-3 Average temperatures** document.

In order to resize the chart object, select it by clicking it, then drag the bottom right-hand handle to the right until the chart reaches the same width as the table, which is **16** cm (or **4** inches). The chart height is changed automatically.

DOCUMENT CONTENTS
Exercise 1.3: Charts

▦ 2. To import data from the first worksheet in the workbook called 1-3 Temperatures in Jacksonville, into the chart you have just created, first double-click the chart to activate Microsoft Graph.

To add this data to the third row of the chart datasheet, click in the first cell on row **3** of the datasheet.
Use **Edit - Import File**, then, in the **Look in** box, select the **MOUS Word 2000 Expert** folder and double-click the **1-3 Temperatures in Jacksonville** workbook. Activate the **Range** option in the **Import** frame and type **A2:M2** in the following text box.
Deactivate the **Overwrite existing cells** option and click **OK**

Leave Microsoft Graph by clicking in the **1-3 Average temperatures** document, outside the chart or datasheet.

▦ 3. To make changes to the chart, first double-click it to open Microsoft Graph.

To change the chart type, use **Chart - Chart Type**. Choose the **Line** chart in the **Chart type** box, then double-click the first **Chart sub-type** on the second row.

In order to add a title, use **Chart - Chart Options**, and click the **Title** tab if necessary. In the **Chart title** text box, type **Average temperatures** then click **OK**.

To show this title in italics, click it in order to select it, then use **Format - Selected Chart Title**. In the **Font Style** list on the **Font** tab, choose the **Italic** option and click **OK**.

To close Microsoft Graph, click outside of the chart and the datasheet, anywhere in the **1-3 Average temperatures** document.

DOCUMENT CONTENTS
Lesson 1.4: Objects

1. Inserting a picture from a file 62

2. Deleting an object 63

3. Moving an object.. 63

4. Sizing an object 64

5. Changing the wrapping of an object.. 64

6. Positioning an object... 67

Practice Exercise 1.4 69

1 ▪ Inserting a picture from a file

* Click in the document where you want to insert the picture.

* **Insert - Picture - From File**

* Go to the drive that contains the picture using the **Look in** list.

* Go to the folder that contains the picture you want to insert by double-clicking the folder icon.

* To see only Bitmap pictures, meaning pictures made up of pixels, select a bitmap format in the **Files of type** list; which may have the extension BMP, PCX, TIF...

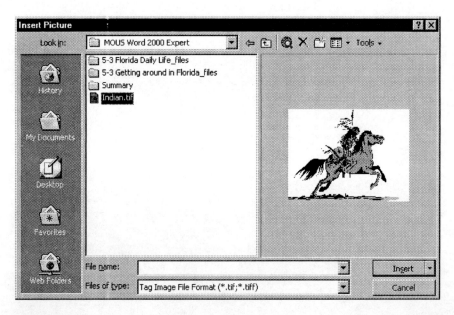

* Select the picture you want to insert.

* Click the **Insert** button.

▥2 ▪ **Deleting an object**

- ▪ Select the object you want to delete.
- ▪ Press Del.

▥3 ▪ **Moving an object**

- ▪ Select the object.
- ▪ Point to the inside of the selection, or to one of the sides if the object is empty or a text box. When the pointer becomes a four-headed arrow, click and drag the object.

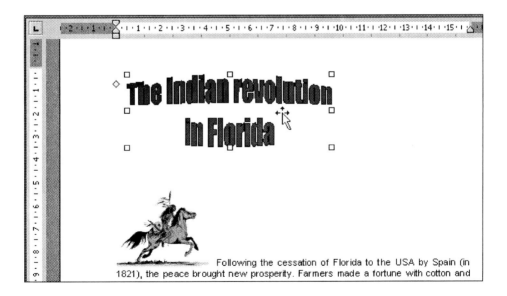

 *If the **Snap objects to grid** option in the **Drawing Grid** dialog box (**Draw - Grid**) is active, the selection is attracted to the lines of a transparent grid.*

4 ▪ Sizing an object

▪ Select the object you want to size.

▪ Drag one of the selection handles.

> 📄 To size an object with precision, use the **Format** dialog box (**Format** - last option in the menu - **Size** tab).

> To size a picture or chart type drawing object whilst keeping its proportions, drag a selection handle on one of the corners. For regular shapes, hold the ⌨Shift key down to resize an object whilst keeping its proportions.

5 ▪ Changing the wrapping of an object

▪ Select the object in question.

▪ Choose the last option in the **Format** menu.

The name of this option depends on the selection: **Picture, Text Box** or **AutoShape**.

▪ Activate the **Layout** tab.

▪ Specify how the text should be distributed around the object by choosing a **Wrapping style**.

▪ Choose the **Horizontal alignment** of the object in relation to the margins.

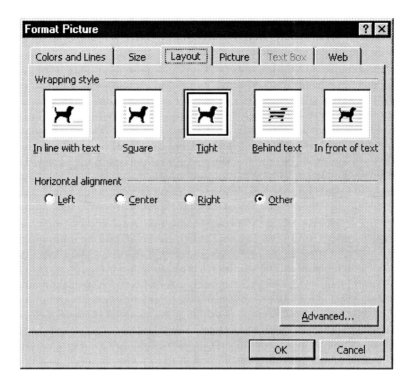

*The **Other** option allows you to align the object using the options in the **Advanced Layout** dialog box, which can be accessed by clicking the **Advanced** button.*

- To define the text wrapping of the object with more precision, click the **Advanced** button, then the **Text Wrapping** tab.

- Choose the **Wrapping style** if you need to.

- In the **Wrap text** frame, indicate how the text should be aligned around the object: on **Both sides**, **Left only**, **Right only** or **Largest only** (to distribute the text along the largest side of the object).

- If necessary, change the **Distance from text**, which is the distance between the sides of the object and the text.

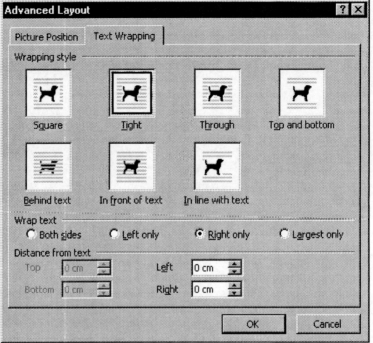

* Click **OK**.

*You return to the **Format** dialog box.*

* Click **OK** again.

📄 *You can open the **Format** dialog box by double-clicking the object (except an embedded object such as a WordArt object).*

🔖 *You can also use the 🐕 tool on the **Picture** toolbar to change the wrapping of an object.*

6 ▪ Positioning an object

» Select the object in question.

» Choose the last option in the **Format** menu.

» Activate the **Layout** tab.

» Click the **Advanced** button, then the **Picture Position** tab.

» In the **Horizontal** frame, click the option that corresponds to the horizontal alignment you want, then use the associated drop-down lists to indicate the reference point for the position of the object. The three options available are:

Alignment	aligns the object to the left, centre or right of the item selected in the **relative to** drop-down list.
Book layout	aligns the object in relation to the inside or outside of the page margin or the page itself.
Absolute position	aligns the object horizontally, respecting the spacing specified between the left side of the object and the left side of the option selected in the **to the left of** drop-down list.

» In the **Vertical** frame, click the option that corresponds to the vertical alignment you want then use the associated drop-down lists to choose the reference point for the alignment. There are two options:

Alignment	aligns the object relative to the top, centre, bottom, inside or outside of the item selected in the **relative to** drop-down list.
Absolute position	aligns the object vertically between the to side of the object and the item selected in the **below** drop-down list, respecting the specified spacing.

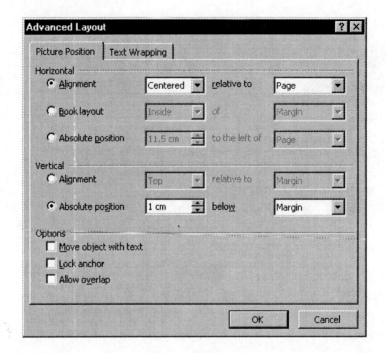

- Define the object attachment options using the check boxes in the **Options** frame:

Move object with text   if this option is active, the object will follow the text to which it is anchored by the top or bottom. If this is the case, you cannot choose an **Absolute Vertical position** relative to the **Page** or the **Margin**.

Lock anchor   activate this option if you want to keep the object in the same position in relation to the same paragraph on the page. A padlock appears above and to the right of the anchor, indicating that the anchor position cannot be changed even if you move the object.

Allow overlap   if this option is active, several objects with the same wrapping can be overlapped.

- Click **OK** twice.

Below, you can see **Practice Exercise** 1.4. This exercise is made up of 6 steps. If you do not know how to complete one of the steps, go back to the lesson to refer to the corresponding title. When you have finished, check your work by reading the **Solution** on the next page.

Steps that are likely to be tested on the exam are marked with a 🏛 symbol. It is however recommended that you follow the whole exercise in order to gain a complete understanding of the lesson.

👉 Practice Exercise 1.4

*In order to complete exercise 1.4, you will need to open **1-4 Florida Indians.doc** in the **MOUS Word 2000 Expert** folder.*

🏛 1. Insert the **Indian.tif** picture from the **MOUS Word 2000 Expert** folder at the beginning of the first paragraph **Following the cessation of Florida...**

🏛 2. Delete the orange AutoShape that looks like a lightning bolt.

🏛 3. Move the **The Indian revolution in Florida** WordArt object so that it is aligned on the left margin of the document.

4. Resize the WordArt object so that its width is approximately **16** cm (**4** inches).

5. Change the wrapping of the picture you have just inserted to achieve the result below:

The Indian revolution in Florida

Following the cessation of Florida to the USA by Spain (in 1821), the peace brought new prosperity. Farmers made a fortune with cotton and tobacco. This was the time when the land in the interior of the state, where the Seminoles lived, was conquered.

These Indians had broken away from the creek peoples, who were from Georgia, to come to Florida in the 18th century. Approximately 4000 Seminoles were living in Florida in 1819. When Spain sold Florida, an article in the contract specified that: "the buyer undertakes to respect the rights of the Indians and

You will need to change the wrapping to leave the least amount of space possible between the object and the text whilst keeping the text to the right of the picture.

6. On page 2, position the picture in order to achieve this layout:

The war ended due to a shortage of soldiers and energy. Several Seminoles left Florida, deported or of their own volition, for Oklahoma; others fled to the marshes, where they would remain. The second Indian war ended on 14th August 1842.

The last episode of this conflict was in 1997: 300 delegates of the Seminole people accepted the 16 million dollars offered in damages by the federal government for the dispossession of 13 million hectares. The war hatchet seems to be well and truly buried.

To do this, you will need to choose a central horizontal alignment in relation to the page, and a vertical position of 1 cm below the top margin.

If you want to put what you have learned into practice in a real document, you can work on the summary exercise 1 for the DOCUMENT CONTENTS section that you can find at the end of this book.

It is often possible to perform a task in several different ways, but here only the quickest solution is presented. Go back to the lesson to see the other techniques that can be used.

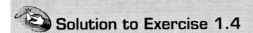

Solution to Exercise 1.4

1. To insert the "Indian.tif" picture at the beginning of the first paragraph "Following the cessation of Florida...", click at the beginning of this paragraph.
   Activate **Insert - Picture - From File**.
   In the **Look in** list, choose the **MOUS Word 2000 Expert** folder, on the drive on which you installed the Word 2000 Expert CD-ROM.
   Click the **Indian.tif** picture and click **Insert**.

2. To delete the orange, lightning bolt AutoShape, select it and press Del.

3. To move the "The Indian revolution in Florida" WordArt object, first click it to select it.
   When the mouse pointer becomes a four-headed arrow, drag the object towards the left in order to align it with the left margin of the document.

4. To resize the WordArt object, select it if necessary.
   Point to the middle handle on the right side of the object and drag to the right until the width reaches 16 cm (4 inches).

DOCUMENT CONTENTS
Exercise 1.4: Objects

5. To change the wrapping of the picture you have just inserted in order to achieve the result shown in step 5 of the exercise, first select the picture.
Use **Format - Picture** and click the **Layout** tab.
In the **Wrapping style** frame, choose **Tight**.
Click the **Advanced** button then the **Text Wrapping** tab to define the text wrapping with more precision.
In the **Wrap text** frame, choose **Right only**.
In the **Distance from text** frame, enter **0** in the **Left** and **Right** text boxes.
Click **OK** twice.

6. To position the picture on page 2 as shown in step 6 of the exercise, click the picture to select it.
Activate **Format - Picture**, then the **Layout** tab. Click the **Advanced** button then the **Picture Position** tab.

To choose to centre the picture horizontally, choose an **Alignment** that is **Centered relative to Page** in the **Horizontal** frame.

To choose a position 1 cm below the top margin, activate the **Absolute position** in the **Vertical** frame, and choose **1 cm below** the **Margin**.
Click **OK** twice.

DOCUMENT PRESENTATION
Lesson 2.1: Formatting paragraphs/pages

1. Applying a fill colour to a paragraph 74

2. Applying a border to pages 74

3. Changing the layout of columns 75

4. Managing line and paragraph breaks 78

5. Creating a watermark 80

6. Applying a particular layout to the first page 81

Practice Exercise 2.1 84

DOCUMENT PRESENTATION
Lesson 2.1: Formatting paragraphs/pages

1 ▪ Applying a fill colour to a paragraph

🖱 ▪ Select the paragraphs in question.

▪ If necessary, show the **Tables and Borders** toolbar by clicking .

▪ Open the list on the tool and choose the fill colour you want.

📋 ▪ Select the paragraphs in question.

▪ **Format - Borders and Shading**, **Shading** tab

▪ Choose the fill colour in the **Fill** frame.

▪ Choose the percentage or the pattern in the **Style** frame.

▪ Choose the pattern colour in the **Color** list.

▪ Click **OK**.

📄 *Generally, this sort of colouring can make the text more difficult to read. Be careful when choosing your colours, and the style and size of the characters.*

2 ▪ Applying a border to pages

▪ Place the insertion point in the section concerned.

▪ **Format - Borders and Shading**, **Page Border** tab.

▪ Under **Setting**, choose the type of border to apply: **Box**, **Shadow**, **3-D** or **Custom**.

*The **Custom** option allows you to apply a different line to each side of the page.*

▪ Choose the **Style** and the **Color** of the line, or choose a border from the **Art** list.

- If necessary, change the **Width** of the border.
- If the border is only to be applied to some sides of the page, use the diagram to click the corresponding sides.

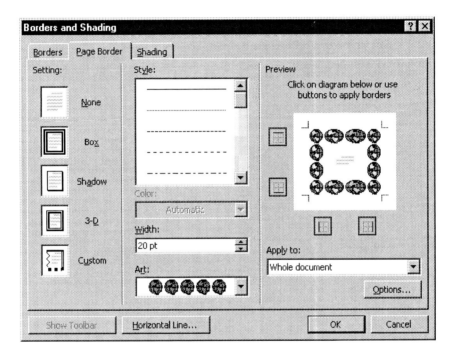

- Indicate which part of the document is to be framed using the **Apply to** drop-down list.
- Click **OK**.

3 • Changing the layout of columns

Inserting a column break

- Place the insertion point at the beginning of the line that is to come after the column break.
- **Insert - Break - Column break** or Ctrl Shift ⏎

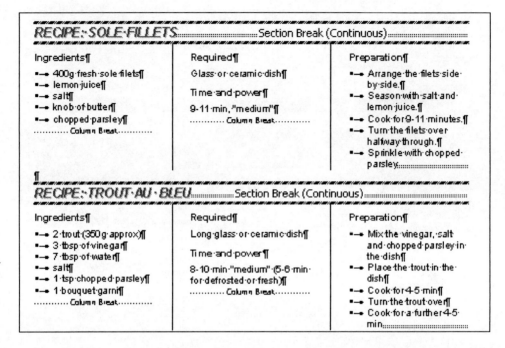

*If the non-printing characters are visible, a dotted line with **Column Break** written on it indicates a column break.*

Changing the column width

- To change the width of columns, you need to be in Print Layout view. Click in one of the columns.

- Drag the column indicators (left or right margin).

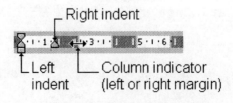

Right indent

Left indent

Column indicator (left or right margin)

If the columns are of equal width, all the columns are modified in the same way; if not, only the column whose width you are changing is modified.

▪ Place the insertion point in the section concerned.

▪ **Format - Columns**

▪ Choose whether all the columns should be of equal width using the **Equal column width** option.

▪ If necessary, change the **Width** and **Spacing** (space between each column) for each or all columns.

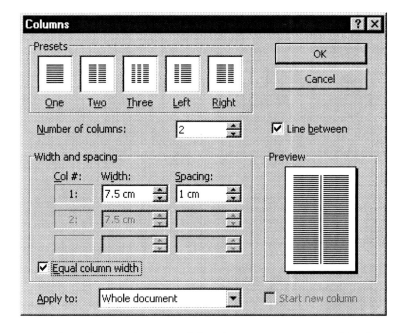

▪ In the **Apply to** list, choose the part of the document concerned by this change.

▪ Click **OK**.

DOCUMENT PRESENTATION
Lesson 2.1: Formatting paragraphs/pages

▣4 ▪ **Managing line and paragraph breaks**

This feature allows you to avoid or create page or column breaks inside a paragraph or between two paragraphs.

▪ Place the insertion point in the paragraph concerned or select the paragraphs.

▪ **Format - Paragraph** or double-click one of the four indent markers on the ruler.

▪ Activate the **Line and Page Breaks** tab.

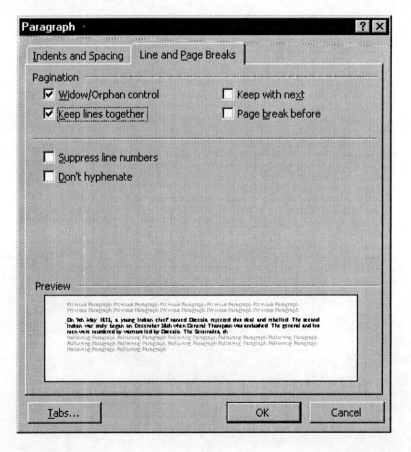

※ In the **Pagination** frame, activate or deactivate the following options:

Widow/Orphan control	Wherever the insertion point is, if this option is active, Word prevents the last line of a paragraph (widow line) from being printed at the top of a page and the first line of a paragraph (orphan line) from being printed at the bottom of a page.
Keep lines together	If this option is active, Word prevents the active paragraph from being broken.
Keep with next	If this option is active, Word will keep the selected paragraph and the one that follows it together; to keep several paragraphs together you need to select all the paragraphs in question except the last one then activate this option.
Page break before	If this option is active, Word inserts a page break before the active paragraph.

※ Click **OK**.

DOCUMENT PRESENTATION
Lesson 2.1: Formatting paragraphs/pages

📖5 ▪ **Creating a watermark**

A watermark is a drawing object (text box, AutoShape, picture) that appears behind or on top of the text in all the pages of a document. For example:

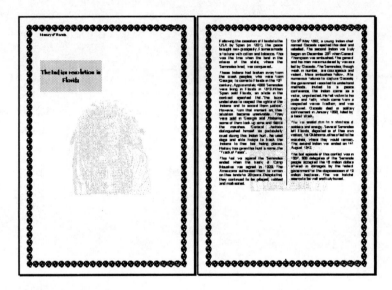

※ Go to the header or footer of the page (**View - Header and Footer**).

※ Click the ⊞ tool on the **Header and Footer** toolbar to hide the contents of the document.

※ Insert the drawing object of your choice.

※ Modify the size and the wrapping of the drawing object using the last option in the **Format** menu or, for a picture, the tools on the **Picture** toolbar.

※ If the watermark is a picture, you can change the image control options by clicking the ⊞ button on the **Picture** toolbar. Choose from:

Automatic   to use the initial colours of the picture.

Grayscale   to turn a colour picture into one using shades of grey.

Black & White   to turn a colour picture black and white.

Watermark   to increase the brightness and dim the colours of the picture.

Be careful, if the colours of the picture are too strong, the text may become illegible.

*You can find these options in the **Format - Picture** dialog box, **Picture** tab, **Color** list in the **Image control** frame.*

■ Once you have made all your changes, click the **Close** button on the **Header and Footer** toolbar.

*If the watermark is a picture, you can use the **Picture** toolbar to make your changes:*

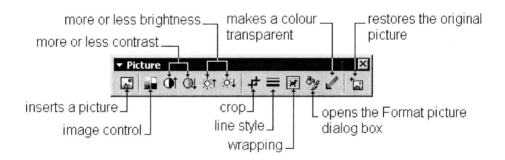

▦6 ▪ Applying a particular layout to the first page

This technique is about creating a specific header/footer or border for the first page of a section or document (if the document contains only one section).

Creating a header/footer for the first page

■ Place the insertion point at the beginning of the document or section in question.

■ **View - Header and Footer**

DOCUMENT PRESENTATION
Lesson 2.1: Formatting paragraphs/pages

* Click the 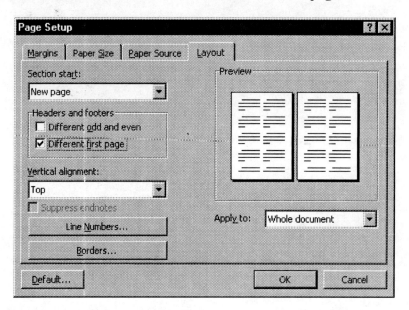 tool on the **Header and Footer** toolbar.

* If necessary, activate the **Layout** tab.

* In the **Headers and footers** frame, activate **Different first page**.

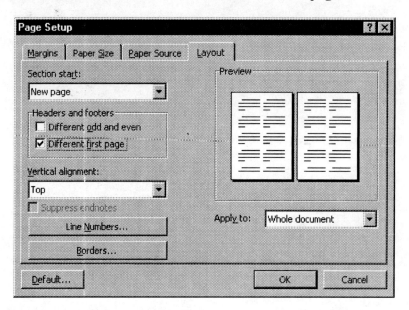

* Click **OK**.

  *A frame called **First Page Header**, followed possibly by **Section [number]** appears. Any existing headers or footers are deleted.*

* Define the header or footer for the first page; use the 🔲 or 🔲 tools to go to the next or previous header/footer if you need to edit it or copy from it.

Creating a page border for the first page

* Place the insertion point at the beginning of the document or section concerned.
* **Format - Borders and Shading**
* Click the **Page Border** tab.

- Define the **Setting**, the **Style**, the **Color** or an option from the **Art** list and the **Width** of the border (see also Applying a border to pages).

- In the **Apply to** list, choose **This section - First page only**.

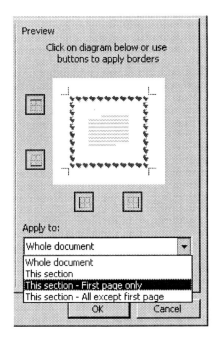

*The **This section - All except first page** option allows you to apply the border to all the pages except the first.*

- Click **OK**.

Only the first page of the section will have this border; you will not be able to apply a different border to the other pages in the section.

 *To apply a specific page layout (columns, orientation, margins, vertical alignment) to certain pages in a document, create a section for these pages, and then use **Format - Columns** or **File - Page Setup**. Having specified the options you want, choose the option **This section** in the **Apply to** list.*

DOCUMENT PRESENTATION
Exercise 2.1: Formatting paragraphs/pages

Below, you can see **Practice Exercise** 2.1. This exercise is made up of 6 steps. If you do not know how to complete one of the steps, go back to the lesson to refer to the corresponding title. When you have finished, check your work by reading the **Solution** on the next page.

All the steps in this exercise are likely to be tested in the exam.

☞ **Practice Exercise 2.1**

*In order to complete exercise 2.1, you will need to open **2-1 Florida Indians** in the **MOUS Word 2000 Expert** folder.*

1. On the first page of the document, apply a **Tan** fill colour to the **The Indian revolution in Florida** paragraph, and the empty paragraphs before and after.

2. Apply a border that represents the "American" side of the globe, 20 points thick, to the document.

3. Change the column width so that the columns have an equal width of 7.5 cm (3 inches) and the spacing is 1 cm.

4. On page 2, prevent the column break in the middle of the paragraph that begins **On 9th May 1832,...**

5. Insert the **Chief.bmp** picture from the **MOUS Word 2000 Expert** folder as a watermark. Choose the **Behind text** wrapping, centre the picture horizontally and vertically in relation to the page, and apply a width of **12 cm** or **4 ¾ inches** (the height should remain in proportion). Use the image control to apply the **Watermark** option. View the pages in Print Preview, and then return to the document.

6. On the first page of the document, insert the text **History of Florida** as a left-aligned header. The watermark you created in the previous step should appear on this first page. Print the document.

If you want to put what you have learned into practice in a real document, you can work on the summary exercise 2 for the DOCUMENT PRESENTATION section that you can find at the end of this book.

DOCUMENT PRESENTATION
Exercise 2.1: Formatting paragraphs/pages

It is often possible to perform a task in several different ways, but here only the quickest solution is presented. Go back to the lesson to see the other techniques that can be used.

 Solution to Exercise 2.1

1. To apply a tan fill colour to the "The Indian revolution in Florida" paragraph, and the previous and following paragraphs, first select these three paragraphs.

   If necessary, show the **Tables and Borders** toolbar by clicking the 🔲 tool. Open the list on the 🪣▾ tool and click the colour **Tan** (at the bottom of the palette, to the left).

2. To apply a border that represents the "American" side of the globe, 20 points thick, to the whole document, activate **Format - Borders and Shading** then the **Page Border** tab.
   In the **Art** list, select the border that shows the globe on the "American" side. Word immediately selects the **Box Setting** for the border.
   In the **Width** box, type **20** then make sure that the **Whole document** is selected in the **Apply to** list.
   Click **OK**.

3. To change the width of the columns so that they are of equal width, activate **Format - Columns**.
   Activate the **Equal column width** choice.
   Instantly, the **Width** of Column 1 is displayed as **7.5 cm** and the **Spacing** is **1 cm**.
   Make sure that **Whole document** is selected in the **Apply to** list and click **OK**.

▦ 4. To prevent the column break in the middle of the paragraph that begins with "On 9th May 1832,...", on page 2, click in this paragraph.
Activate **Format - Paragraph** and click the **Line and Page Breaks** tab.
Activate the **Keep lines together** option and click **OK**.

▦ 5. To insert the Chief.bmp picture from the MOUS Word 2000 Expert folder as a watermark, use **View - Header and Footer**. Click the ▦ tool to hide the document text.
Activate **Insert - Picture - From File**. In the **Look in** list, select the **MOUS Word 2000 Expert** folder and double-click the **Chief.bmp** picture.

To change the wrapping and size of the picture, click it to select it then use **Format - Picture**.
Activate the **Layout** tab then select the **Behind text Wrapping style**. Click the **Advanced** button, and in the **Horizontal** frame on the **Picture Position** tab, select an **Alignment Centered relative to Page**. In the **Vertical** frame, select an **Alignment Centered relative to Page**, then click **OK**.
Activate the **Size** tab, and, in the **Size and rotate** frame, specify a **Width** of **12 cm**.

To apply a "Watermark" image control setting, activate the **Picture** tab, open the **Color** list in the **Image control** frame and select **Watermark**.
Click **OK** to close the **Format Picture** dialog box then **Close** on the **Header and Footer** toolbar.

Click the ▦ tool to see a print preview of the document. Scroll the pages then click **Close** to return to the document.

6. To insert a left-aligned header on the first page of the document, containing the text "History of Florida", press ⌨Ctrl⌨🔙 to go to the beginning of the document. Activate **View - Header and Footer** then click the 🔲 tool on the **Header and Footer** toolbar to hide the document text.

Click the 📖 tool on the **Header and Footer** toolbar then activate the **Layout** tab if you need to. In the **Headers and footers** frame, activate the **Different first page** option and click **OK**.
Press ↵ then type **History of Florida**.

To insert the watermark you created previously into the first page, click the 🔳 tool, then the watermark picture, then 📑 to copy the picture to the clipboard. Return to the first header by clicking 🔳 and insert the picture by clicking 📋.

Finish by clicking the **Close** button on the **Header and Footer** toolbar then click the 🖨 tool to print the document.

DOCUMENT PRESENTATION
Lesson 2.2: Styles and templates

1. Creating a style 90

2. Applying a style 93

3. Managing styles 95

4. Creating a document template 99

5. Modifying a template 101

6. Linking a template to an existing document 102

Practice Exercise 2.2 104

DOCUMENT PRESENTATION
Lesson 2.2: Styles and templates

🗐 1 ▪ Creating a style

A style contains character and/or paragraph formatting. Creating a style allows you to save a certain presentation and apply it later. Styles are saved in the document or template.

Based on existing formatting

▪ Open, if necessary, the template or document in question.

▪ Apply the formatting you want to save in the style.

▪ Place the insertion point in the paragraph you have formatted.

▪ Click the name of the active style in the **Style** list on the **Formatting** toolbar.

▪ Enter the name of the new style then press ↵.

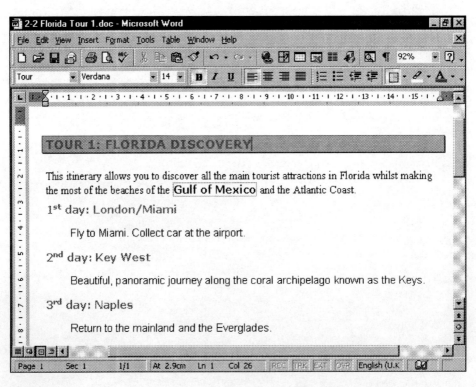

The style is immediately applied to the active paragraph.

📄 *Using this technique means that you cannot assign a shortcut key, nor create a character style.*

Without existing formatting

▪ **Format - Style**

▪ Click the **New** button and type the name of the style in the **Name** box.

▪ If the style you are creating is only for characters, select the **Character** option in the **Style type** list.

▪ In the **Based on** list, choose an existing style on which to base your style, if you want to.

▪ In the **Style for following paragraph** list, choose the style that you want to be applied to the next paragraph as you type. When you press ⏎ after typing text in the new style, Word will automatically apply the style you choose in this list.

▪ Use the options in the list on the **Format** button to define the presentation of your style.

▪ If necessary, click the **Shortcut Key** button, activate the **Press new shortcut key** text box, and press your shortcut key on the keyboard.

▪ Make sure that **[unassigned]** appears underneath **Currently assigned to**.

▪ Use the **Save changes in** list to choose the document or template in which this shortcut key can be used to apply the style.

DOCUMENT PRESENTATION
Lesson 2.2: Styles and templates

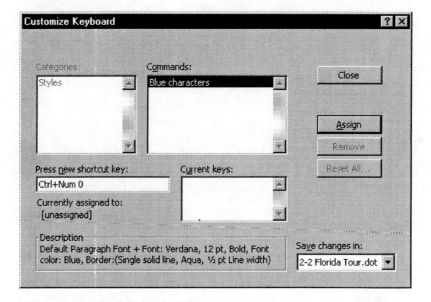

» Click the **Assign** button then the **Close** button to leave the dialog box.

You return to the New Style dialog box.

» Activate the **Add to template** option if you are not working in a template and you want to create the style in the template associated with the active document (and not just in the document).

» Activate **Automatically update** if any changes made to a paragraph to which the style is applied will cause the style to be updated to include these changes.

This option is not available for character styles.

※ Click **OK** to close the **New Style** dialog box.

※ Once you have finished creating your styles, click the **Close** button in the **Style** dialog box.

2 ▪ Applying a style

This action allows you to apply a saved style to your text.

※ To apply a character style, select the text in question; to apply a paragraph style, select the paragraphs or click in the paragraph in question.

※ Open the **Style** list on the **Formatting** toolbar.

DOCUMENT PRESENTATION
Lesson 2.2: Styles and templates

denotes a paragraph style   denotes a character style

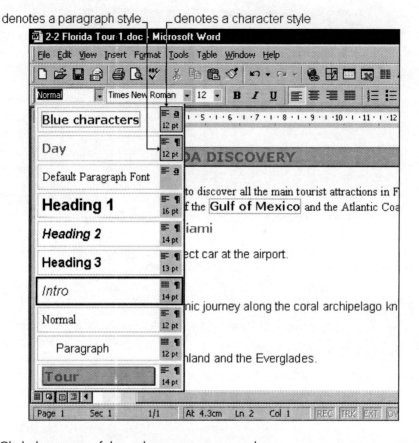

※ Click the name of the style you want to apply.

The automatic formatting of the style is applied instantly.

※ If necessary, select the text you want to format.

※ Type the shortcut key defined when the style was created.

📄 *To apply a style, you can also use **Format - Style**, click the name of the style you want to use in the **Styles** list and click the **Apply** button.*

Using a style does not put any limits on the formatting of text. You can still add formatting to your characters and/or paragraphs.

To undo a character style, apply the **Default Paragraph Font**; to undo a paragraph style, apply the **Normal** style or press ⌈Ctrl⌋⌈Shift⌋ *N*.

▥3 • Managing styles

Modifying a style

- Activate the document or template that contains the style in question.
- Make the formatting changes in text to which the style is applied.
- Click the name of the style you want to modify in the **Styles** list on the **Formatting** toolbar and press ↵.

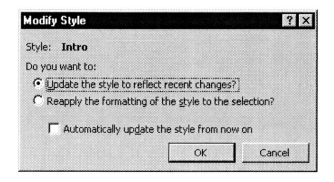

Word asks you whether or not you want to update the style with the changes.

- Leave the **Update the style to reflect recent changes** option and click **OK**.

 *If you activate the **Automatically update the style from now on** option, the **Modify Style** dialog box will no longer appear and the styles will be updated systematically.*
This technique does not allow you to update the style in the template (unless you are working directly in the template).

DOCUMENT PRESENTATION
Lesson 2.2: Styles and templates

■ * Activate the document or the template that contains the style you want to change.

■ * **Format - Style**

■ * In the **Styles** list, select the style you want to change.

■ * Click the **Modify** button.

■ * Change the characteristics of the style using the choices in the list on the **Format** button.

■ * If you are not working in the template, but in a document based on the template and you want to change the template style, activate the **Add to template** option.

■ * Click **OK**.

■ * Make any changes to other styles in the same way then click **Close**.

*To change the standard appearance of paragraphs, make changes to the style called **Normal**.*

Deleting a style

■ * Open the document or template concerned.

■ * **Format - Style**

■ * Click the name of the style in the **Styles** list.

■ * Click the **Delete** button.

■ * Confirm the deletion with **OK**.

■ * Click **Close**.

*The style is not deleted in existing documents associated with the template. **Normal, Heading 1, Heading 2, Heading 3** are styles created by Word in the Normal.dot template and you cannot delete them in your own templates.*

Printing a list of styles

* Open the template or the document that contains the styles you want to print.

* **File - Print** or `Ctrl` **P**

* Open the **Print what** drop-down list and choose **Styles**.

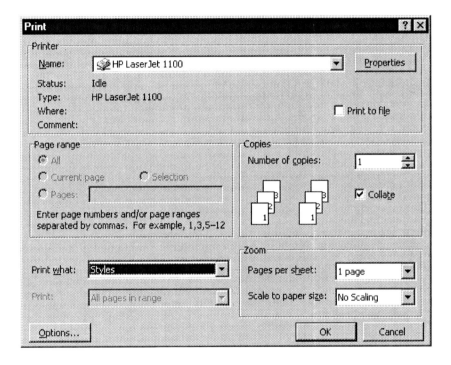

* Click **OK**.

  The styles are printed in alphabetical order with all their characteristics.

DOCUMENT PRESENTATION
Lesson 2.2: Styles and templates

Displaying the styles in a document

* **Tools - Options - View** tab

* Enter a value in the **Style area width** box.

* If necessary, change to **Normal** view.

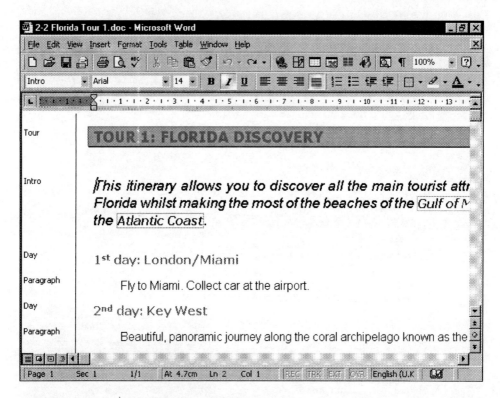

In Normal view, the styles used in each paragraph are shown in the left of the screen.

4 ▪ Creating a document template

A document template allows you to save paragraph and/or character styles in order to automate your work. All new documents are based on the Normal.dot template by default.

You can create a new template, creating your own styles, text as your go... You can also create a template using a document that already contains styles and for text.

Creating a template based on an existing template

» **File - New**

Do not use either the 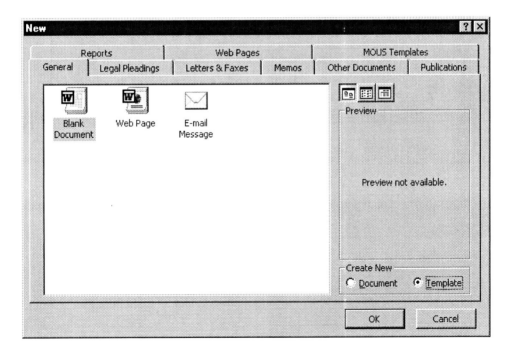 *button or the* Ctrl *N shortcut key, as neither of these will open the **New** dialog box.*

» Click the **Template** option in the **Create New** frame.

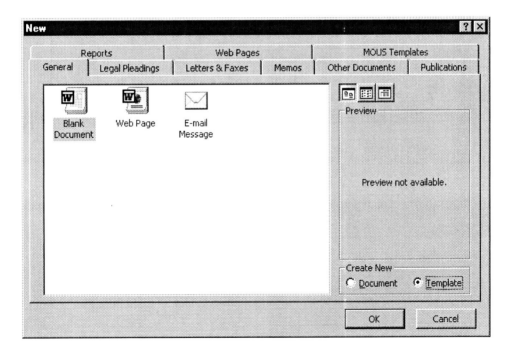

DOCUMENT PRESENTATION
Lesson 2.2: Styles and templates

- If you want to base your new template on the Normal.dot template, make sure that the **Blank Document** icon is selected under the **General** tab. If not, activate the appropriate tab and click the icon of the template you want to use as a base.

- Click **OK**.

  The title bar tells you that you are creating a new template.

- Define the styles, texts... you want to include in the template.

- **File - Save** or ⊞ or ⌈Ctrl⌉ **S**

- Give the template a name.

  The extension given to templates is .dot.

- Click the **Save** button.

  📄 *Templates you create are saved in the **Templates** folder (C:\Windows\Application Data\Microsoft\Templates) of the folder that contains Microsoft Office (or in sub-folder of Templates).*
  *The preset Word templates are not stored in the same **Templates** folder but in sub-folders of a different **Templates** folder (C:\Program Files\Microsoft Office\Templates).*

Creating a template based on an existing document

- If necessary, open the document in question.

- Add your styles, AutoTexts...

- Delete everything you do not want to appear in the template.

- **File - Save As**

- In the **Save as type** drop-down list, choose **Document Template (*.dot)**.

  *Word suggests the **Templates** folder as the default folder.*

- If you do not want to save your template in the Templates folder, choose the appropriate folder.

- If necessary, change the **File name**.

- Click **Save**.

5 • Modifying a template

When you modify a template, you need to open it in order to make your changes.

- **File - Open** or 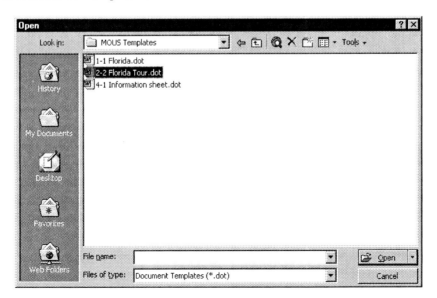 or Ctrl O

- Open the **Files of type** drop-down list and choose **Document Templates (*.dot)**.

The display changes from documents to templates.

- Activate the folder in which the templates are stored (by default: **C:\Windows\Application Data\Microsoft\Templates**) and, if necessary, one of the subfolders of **Templates**.

- Double-click the name of the template you want to open.

- Make your changes then save the template.

📄 When you next want to open a document, you will need to change the *Files of type* option back to *Word Documents (*.doc)*.
The changes you made to the styles are updated in existing documents based on the template.

6 ▪ Linking a template to an existing document

This will enable you to use styles from a template other than the one with which you created the active document.

- **Tools - Templates and Add-Ins**

- Click the **Attach** button in the **Document template** frame.

A list of all document templates appears.

- If you need to, double-click the folder that contains the template.

- Double-click the template you want to use.

- Activate the **Automatically update document styles** choice if you want to update the styles in the document so that they are identical to those in the template.

* Click **OK**.

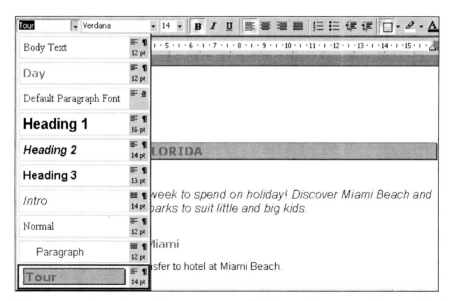

*The **Style** drop-down list contains all the styles currently attached to the document.*

* Apply the template styles as it suits you.

DOCUMENT PRESENTATION
Exercise 2.2: Styles and templates

Below, you can see **Practice Exercise** 2.2. This exercise is made up of 6 steps. If you do not know how to complete one of the steps, go back to the lesson to refer to the corresponding title. When you have finished, check your work by reading the **Solution** on the next page.

Steps that are likely to be tested on the exam are marked with a ▦ symbol. It is however recommended that you follow the whole exercise in order to gain a complete understanding of the lesson.

👉 Practice Exercise 2.2

---

*In order to complete exercise 2.2, you will need to open **2-2 Florida Tour 1.doc** in the **MOUS Word 2000 Expert** folder.*

▦ 1. Create a style called **Tour** based on the appearance of the paragraph **TOUR 1: FLORIDA DISCOVERY**.

2. Apply the **Intro** style to the paragraph that begins **This itinerary....** In this paragraph, apply the **Blue characters** style to the text **Atlantic Coast**.

▦ 3. Modify the **Intro** style by applying a justified paragraph alignment. Save the document.

4. Using the open document as a base, create a document template that contains only the styles. Save the template in the **MOUS Templates** folder in the **Templates** folder and call it **2-2 Florida Tour.dot**. Close the document template.

5. Change the **2-2 Florida Tour.dot** template by deleting the **Blue characters** style. Save and close the template.

6. Open the **2-2 Florida Tour 2.doc** document in the **MOUS Word 2000 Expert** folder and attach the **2-2 Florida Tour.dot** template you have just created. When you attach the template, choose to update the document styles automatically, and then apply styles as follows:

Paragraphs concerned:	Style to be applied:
TOUR 2: FAST FLORIDA	Tour
You have only one week...	Intro
1st day: London/Miami	Day
Fly to Miami...	Paragraph

If you want to put what you have learned into practice in a real document, you can work on the summary exercise 2 for the DOCUMENT PRESENTATION section that you can find at the end of this book.

DOCUMENT PRESENTATION
Exercise 2.2: Styles and templates

It is often possible to perform a task in several different ways, but here only the quickest solution is presented. Go back to the lesson to see the other techniques that can be used.

 Solution to Exercise 2.2

1. To create a style based on the appearance of the "TOUR 1: FLORIDA DISCOVERY" paragraph, first click in this paragraph.
   Click the name of the active style (**Normal**) in the **Style** drop-down list on the **Formatting** toolbar and type **Tour**. Confirm the creation by pressing ⏎.

2. To apply the Intro style to the paragraph that begins "This itinerary...", click in this paragraph then open the **Style** drop-down list on the **Formatting** toolbar and click the **Intro** style.
   To apply the Blue characters style to the text "Atlantic Coast", select **Atlantic Coast**, open the **Style** drop-down list on the **Formatting** toolbar and click **Blue characters**.

3. To change the Intro style click in the "This itinerary..." paragraph, to which this style is applied, and click the ▤ tool to apply a justified paragraph alignment.
   Click in the **Style** drop-down list on the **Formatting** toolbar, choose **Intro**, and press ⏎.
   Click **OK** in the **Modify Style** dialog box.

   To save the document, click 💾.

4. To use the open document to create a document template containing only styles, select the entire document contents using **Edit - Select All** then delete the selection by pressing Del.

Activate **File - Save As** and in the **Save as type** drop-down list, choose **Document Template (*.dot)**.
Double-click the **MOUS Templates** folder.
In the **File name** box, type **2-2 Florida Tour.dot** then click **Save**.
To close the template, use **File - Close**.

5. To make changes to the template by deleting the Blue characters style, open the template. Click the tool, and in the **Files of type** list, choose **Document Templates (*.dot)**, use the **Look in** list to open **C:\Windows\Application Data\Microsoft\Templates** then double-click the **MOUS Templates** folder. Finally, double-click **2-2 Florida Tour.dot**.

To delete the Blue characters style, use **Format - Style**. In the **Styles** list, click **Blue characters** then click the **Delete** button. Confirm this action by clicking **Yes**, and close the dialog box by clicking **Close**.

To save and close the template, use **File - Close** and click **Yes**.

6. To open 2-2 Florida Tour 2.doc and attach the template you created previously, click the tool. In the **Files of type** list, choose **Word Documents (*.doc)** and select the **MOUS Word 2000 Expert** folder using the **Look in** list. Double-click **2-2 Florida Tour 2.doc** to open it.

Activate **Tools - Templates and Add-Ins**. Click the **Attach** button in the **Document template** frame. Double-click the **MOUS Templates** folder and then the **2-2 Florida Tour.dot** template.
Activate the **Automatically update document styles** option then click **OK**.

DOCUMENT PRESENTATION
Exercise 2.2: Styles and templates

Apply the template styles to the first paragraphs as shown below. For each paragraph, click inside the paragraph then open the **Style** drop-down list to select the appropriate style.

Paragraphs concerned:	Style to be applied:
TOUR 2: FAST FLORIDA	Tour
You have only one week...	Intro
1st day: London/Miami	Day
Fly to Miami...	Paragraph

LONG DOCUMENTS
Lesson 3.1: Notes and bookmarks

1. Creating footnotes and endnotes 110

2. Using the notes pane 112

3. Managing existing notes 113

4. Modifying notes 113

5. Working with bookmarks 115

6. Creating cross-references 116

Practice Exercise 3.1 118

LONG DOCUMENTS
Lesson 3.1: Notes and bookmarks

▓1 ▪ Creating footnotes and endnotes

▪ Place the insertion point where you want to insert the note.

▪ **Insert - Footnote**

▪ Choose whether you want to insert a **Footnote** or an **Endnote**.

▪ Choose:

AutoNumber   to leave Word to manage the numbering of the notes.

Mark   to create your own note marks.

Custom marks cannot contain more than 10 characters.

▪ Click **OK**.

If you are in Print Layout view, the insertion point appears at the bottom of the page. A separating line appears between the document text and that of the note.

▪ Type the note contents.

The style used for footnotes is called "Footnote Text", that for note marks is called "Footnote Reference".

▪ Click in the workspace or press F6 (if you are in Normal view).

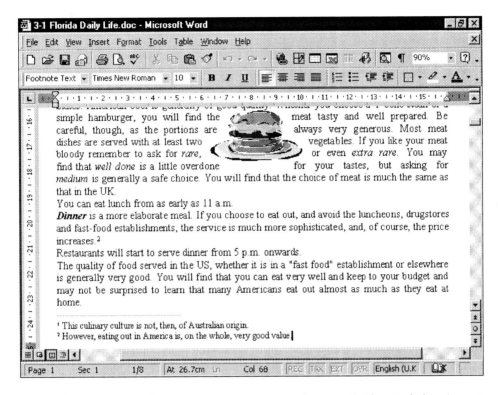

> To see the contents of a note, point to the reference (without clicking) or, in Normal view, use the notes pane.

*If you use the first technique, the note appears in a ScreenTip, if the corresponding option in the **View** tab of the **Tools - Options** dialog box is active.*

Word leaves a space for footnotes at the bottom of each page so that notes are printed on the same page as their marker.

*To move from note to note, use the **Select Browse Object** button then the ⊞ or ⊞ choices to go to footnotes and endnotes respectively.*

2 ▪ Using the notes pane

▪ View - Normal

▪ To open the notes pane, activate the **Footnotes** option in the **View** menu or double-click the note reference.

▪ To change the height of the notes pane, drag the top border of the pane.

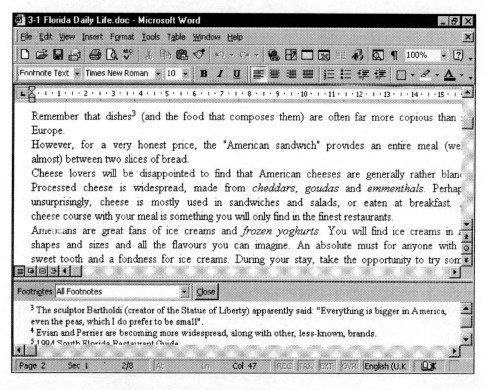

▪ To move quickly between note references, click the text of the corresponding note, then the reference in the document.

▪ To close the notes pane, deactivate the **Footnotes** option in the **View** menu, or click the **Close** button on the notes pane.

▦3 ▪ Managing existing notes

To manage the notes, you need to work with the references and not the note contents.

▪ To change the contents of a note in **Print Layout** view, double-click the note reference then make your changes.

▪ To delete a note, select the marker and press `Del`.

▪ To move a note, simply move the reference as you would a passage of the text.

📄 *If you have chosen to use automatic numbering, the notes will be renumbered automatically.*

▦4 ▪ Modifying notes

Changing the appearance of notes

▪ Depending on the notes you are using, modify the styles **Footnote Reference**, **Endnote Reference**, **Footnote Text** and **Endnote Text** to make changes to the appearance of your notes.

Changing where the notes are printed

▪ **Insert - Footnote**

▪ Click the **Options** button, and activate the tab that corresponds to the notes you are working with.

▪ In the **Place at** drop-down list, indicate where the note is to be printed:

	Position:	Notes printed:
For footnotes	**Bottom of page**	Above the bottom margin
	Beneath text	Below the last line of text on the page
For endnotes	**End of section**	At the end of the section
	End of document	At the end of the document

▪ Click **OK**.

▪ Close the dialog box by clicking **Close** or **OK** if you want to create a new note.

Changing the numbering of notes

▪ **Insert - Footnote**

▪ Click the **Options** button.

▪ Use the **Number format** list to choose the characters you want to use.

▪ To change the first number, type the number you want in the **Start at** box.

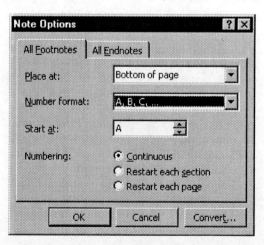

This technique will eliminate redundant numbers when you split a document into several files.

- Indicate whether the **Numbering** should be **Continuous** or **Restart each section** or **Restart each page**.

- Click **OK**.

- Leave the dialog box by clicking **Close** or **OK** to insert a new note.

5 ▪ Working with bookmarks

A bookmark allows you to mark a place in the text so that you can go to it quickly.

Creating a bookmark

- If you want to select text when you go to a bookmark, select the text in question. If you simply want to move the insertion point, place the insertion point where the bookmark is to be.

- **Insert - Bookmark** or [Ctrl][Shift][F5]

- Enter the name of the new bookmark in the **Bookmark name** box.

A bookmark name can be up to 20 characters long, must start with a letter and cannot contain any spaces.

Deleting a bookmark

- **Insert - Bookmark** or [Ctrl][Shift][F5]

- Select the name of the bookmark you want to delete in the **Bookmark name** list.

- Click **Delete** then **Close**.

LONG DOCUMENTS
Lesson 3.1: Notes and bookmarks

Using a bookmark

▪ **Insert - Bookmark** or `Ctrl` `Shift` `F5`

▪ If necessary, change the way the list of existing bookmarks is sorted : choose **Sort by Name** to sort in alphabetical order or **Location** to list them in the order in which they appear in the document.

▪ Double-click the bookmark you want to go, or select it and click **Go To**.

▪ Close the dialog box by clicking **Close**.

 *You can also go to bookmarks by using **Edit - Go To**.*

6 ▪ Creating cross-references

A cross-reference refers to an item (title, footnote, bookmark, legend...), which is elsewhere in the document.

▪ At the appropriate place in the document, type the cross-reference text.

▪ **Insert - Cross-reference**

▪ In the **Reference type** drop-down list, choose the type of element to which you want to refer.

▪ In the **Insert reference to** drop-down list, choose the information you want to insert in the document (the cross-reference).

The content of this list depends on the type of reference you have chosen.

▪ In the **For** list, select the item to which your cross-reference refers.

▪ Activate the **Insert as hyperlink** option if you want to be able to go to the item by clicking the cross-reference.

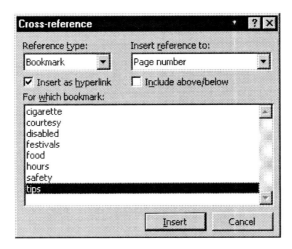

- Activate the **Include above/below** option if you want to add the words **above** or **below** to your cross-reference.

- Click **Insert**.

- If necessary, define any other cross-references.

- Leave the **Cross-reference** dialog box by clicking **Close**.

 *To change the reference of a cross-reference, select the cross-reference and open the **Cross-reference** dialog box (**Insert - Cross-reference**) and choose the new item in the **Insert reference to** drop-down list.*

*To update a cross-reference, select it, or the whole document if you are updating all the references, right-click the selection and choose to **Update Fields**.*

Exercise 3.1: Notes and bookmarks

Below, you can see **Practice Exercise** 3.1. This exercise is made up of 6 steps. If you do not know how to complete one of the steps, go back to the lesson to refer to the corresponding title. When you have finished, check your work by reading the **Solution** on the next page.

Steps that are likely to be tested on the exam are marked with a 🏛 symbol. It is however recommended that you follow the whole exercise in order to gain a complete understanding of the lesson.

☞ Practice Exercise 3.1

In order to complete exercise 3.1, you will need to open **3-1 Florida Daily Life.doc** in the MOUS **Word 2000 Expert** folder.

🏛 1. Create the following footnotes (the notes should be numbered automatically):

Text	Note contents
barbecue (page 1)	This culinary culture is not, then, of Australian origin.
increases (page 1)	However, eating out in America is, on the whole, very good value.

2. Open the notes pane; go to the reference for note no. **3** then close the notes pane. Activate Print Layout view.

🏛 3. Move the marker for note no. **3** to after the word **Europe** in the same sentence then delete note no. **5** (page 4).

4. Change the style **Footnote Text** so that all the notes have a hanging indent of **0.25 cm**.
Change the position of the notes so that they are printed at the bottom of each page containing a note reference.

5. Create the bookmark **hours**, which will send the insertion point to the beginning of the text **OPENING HOURS** on page **7**.
Delete the **sandwich** bookmark, then go to the text that talks about courtesy using the **courtesy** bookmark.

6. After the text **Restaurants will start to serve dinner from 5 p.m. onwards.** (page 1), create a cross-reference that refers to the **tip** bookmark. The introduction text for the reference is: **See also TIPS on page** `Space`. The information you want to insert in the document is the **Page number** and you should be able to go to the **tips** bookmark by clicking the cross-reference.

If you want to put what you have learned into practice in a real document, you can work on the summary exercise 3 for the LONG DOCUMENTS section that you can find at the end of this book.

Exercise 3.1: Notes and bookmarks

It is often possible to perform a task in several different ways, but here only the quickest solution is presented. Go back to the lesson to see the other techniques that can be used.

Solution to Exercise 3.1

 1. To create the first footnote described in step 1, click in page 1 after the word "barbecue", then **Insert - Footnote**.
Leave the **Footnote** and **AutoNumber** options active and click **OK**.
Type **This culinary culture is not, then, of Australian origin**.

To create the second footnote in step 1, click in page 1 after the word "increases", then **Insert - Footnote**.
Leave the **Footnote** and **Automatic** options active and click **OK**.
Type **However, eating out in America is, on the whole, very good value**.

2. In order to open the notes pane, use **View - Normal**, then **View - Footnotes**.

To go to note no. 3, click the text of note no. **3** in the notes pane, then on the note marker in the document.

Close the notes pane by clicking the **Close** button.

To return to Print Layout view, use **View - Print Layout**.

3. Move note no. 3 to after the word "Europe" by selecting the marker of note no. **3**.

   Click the [✄] tool, click after the word **Europe** and click [📋].

   To delete note no. 5, select the note no. **5** reference (on page 4) then press [Del].

4. To change the **Footnote Text** style by applying a hanging indent of 0.25 cm to all the footnotes, click in the text of note no. 3 (page 2).
   On the ruler, drag the hanging indent marker to **0.25 cm** to achieve the following result:

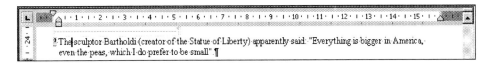

   Open the **Style** drop-down list on the **Formatting** toolbar and click the style **Footnote Text**.
   Leave the **Update style to reflect recent changes** option active and click **OK**.

   Change the position of the notes so that they are printed at the bottom of the page by using **Insert - Footnote**, then click the **Options** button.
   Open the **Place at** drop-down list and choose **Bottom of page**.
   Click **OK** then **Close**.

5. To create the "hours" bookmark, click at the beginning of the title **OPENING HOURS** on page **7** and use **Insert - Bookmark**.
   Type **hours** in the **Bookmark name** box and click **Add**.

   Delete the "sandwich" bookmark by activating **Insert - Bookmark** selecting the word **sandwich** in the **Bookmark name** list, then clicking **Delete** followed by **Close**.

   To go to the text that discusses courtesy, use **Insert - Bookmark**, and double-click **courtesy** in the **Bookmark name** list, then click **Close**.

6. To create a cross-reference that refers to the "tip" bookmark, click after the text "Restaurants will start to serve dinner from 5 p.m. onwards.", press `Space` then type **See also TIPS on page** `Space`.

Use **Insert - Cross-reference**, select **Bookmark** in the **Reference type** list and **Page number** in the **Insert reference to** list.

In the **For which bookmark** list, choose **tips**, leave the **Insert as hyperlink** option active then click **Insert** followed by **Close**.

LONG DOCUMENTS
Lesson 3.2: Outlines and tables

1. Creating an outline using preset styles 124

2. Applying an outline level to a paragraph 125

3. Using the document outline 127

4. Creating a table of contents from an outline 128

5. Updating a table of contents 129

6. Creating an index 130

7. Updating an index 132

Practice Exercise 3.2 133

1 • Creating an outline using preset styles

■ Activate **Outline** view.

■ **View - Outline** or

The Outlining bar replaces the ruler and each paragraph is preceded by an empty square.

■ To enter a heading in an outline, apply preset styles according to the importance of the heading:

Heading 1 principal headings,

Heading 2 subheadings,

Heading 3   for sub-subheadings.

*You can apply preset styles in other views than Outline view. The **Heading 1, Heading 2** and **Heading 3** styles remove your own formatting. If you want to keep your own formatting, you will need to redefine these styles. If a cross precedes text, it is a heading in the outline.*

* Once you have entered a heading in the outline, you can promote it by one level, using the [←] button, or use [→] to demote it.

 *If a normal text has been defined as a heading by accident, undo this by applying a style other than **Heading 1, Heading 2, Heading 3**...*

Leave Outline view by changing the view.

If paragraphs in your document contain custom styles that you want to keep, you need to apply an outline level to each style if you want to create an outline.

2 ▪ Applying an outline level to a paragraph

If you want to create a table of contents or number your headings automatically, but do not want to lose your custom formatting, you need to apply an outline level to all your paragraphs (or paragraph styles).

To a paragraph

* Place the insertion point in the paragraph concerned, or select it.

* **Format - Paragraph - Indents and Spacing** tab

* In the **Outline level** list, choose the level you want to apply (from 1 to 9) to the paragraph.

* Click **OK**.

* Define the outline level for each paragraph in this way.

To a paragraph style

⬚ **Format - Style**

⬚ In the **Styles** list, select the style to which you want to apply an outline level.

⬚ Click the **Modify** button.

⬚ Click the **Format** button and choose the **Paragraph** option.

⬚ In the **Outline level** list, choose from levels 1 to 9 for this paragraph style.

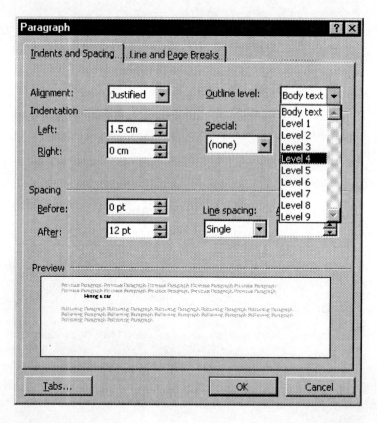

⬚ Click **OK** twice then **Close**.

3 ▪ Using the document outline

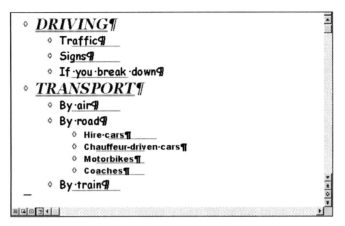

※ Go to **Outline** view by **View - Outline**

※ Make your choice, keeping the following principles in mind:

To	🖰	🎲
Show all headings from one level and any higher levels	buttons **1** to **7**	**Alt** **Shift** and the number (main keyboard)
Show the whole document (headings and text)	**All** button	
Hide the text linked to a heading	double-click the cross before the heading or click **—**	press - (number pad)
Show the text linked to a heading	double-click the cross before the heading or click **+**	
Promote a heading	◆	**Alt** **Shift** ←
Demote a heading	◆	**Alt** **Shift** →

※ To print the document outline, show only the headings then print.

LONG DOCUMENTS
Lesson 3.2: Outlines and tables

The whole document is shown in print preview, even though only the headings will be printed.

* To move a heading, with any associated subheadings and text, point to the cross that precedes the heading and drag it to the new position, or click in the heading and use ⬆ or ⬇.

4 ▪ Creating a table of contents from an outline

* Place the insertion point where you want to insert the table of contents.
* **Insert - Index and Tables**
* Activate the **Table of Contents** tab.
* In the **Formats** list in the **General** frame, choose the presentation you want and check the result in the **Print Preview** frame.

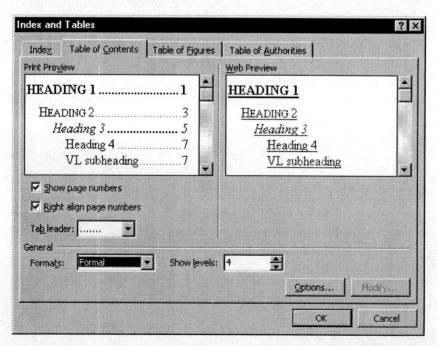

* If you wish, indicate which items are to appear and how. If you want to **Show page numbers**, you need to decide whether you want to **Right align page numbers**. Decide how many levels you want to show in the **Show levels** list.

* For all presentations except **Simple** and **Modern**, you can choose the **Tab leader**.

* Click **OK**.

* If necessary, use [Alt][F9] to hide the codes for the table of contents you have created and visualise the result.

  For each heading in the table of contents, a hyperlink is created.

* To go to a heading, click the corresponding entry in the table of contents.

  The table uses the styles TOC 1, TOC 2,..., which you can, of course, change. To change the appearance of the table of contents, select another ***Format*** *in the* ***Table of Contents*** *tab in the* ***Index and Tables*** *dialog box (**Insert - Index and Tables**). The new format will replace the old one after you confirm the change.*
  You should always be sure that the page numbers in your document will not change before inserting a table of contents.

⊞5 ▪ Updating a table of contents

* Click before one the headings in the table to activate it.

  The grey background indicates the table is active.

* Press [F9].

* Choose to **Update page numbers only** or **Update entire table**.

* Click **OK**.

LONG DOCUMENTS
Lesson 3.2: Outlines and tables

6 ▪ Creating an index

Here is an example of an index:

B		**M**
Breakdown.........................4		Motorbike
		Hire.............................6
C		Motoribike
		Travelling......................6
Car		
Chauffeur driven..............6		**P**
Cost.........................6		
Fuel.........................6		Petrol
Hire car conditions 5		Car..............................6
Hire car details............5		Plane............................7
How to hire a car...........5		
Cars		**R**
American cars...............4		
Coach		Road
Travelling 6		Transport....................5
Cost		
Hire car.....................6		**S**
D		Signs
Driving		Junctions....................3

Defining an index entry

* If the entry exists already, select it, otherwise, place the insertion point where the subject of the entry is.

* **Insert - Index and Tables - Index** tab - **Mark Entry** button or Alt Shift X

* If necessary, type the **Main entry** in the appropriate box.

* If necessary, go to the **Subentry** box and type the subentry.

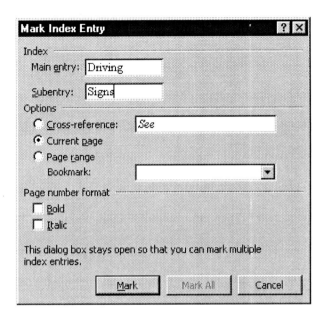

- If other entry levels need to be created, type a colon (:) before entering the rest of the text in the **Subentry** box.

- Activate the **Cross-reference** option if you want to add a cross-reference rather than a page number.

- Activate the **Current page** option to show the number of the page containing the selected index entry.

- Activate the **Page range** option to select, in the **Bookmark** list, the bookmark that signals the end of the page range for the entry.

- If necessary, format the text you have entered using shortcut keys.

- Confirm by pressing **Mark** then **Close**.

    You can see the entry field {XE...}, which is hidden text, if you are displaying special characters.

Inserting an index

* Hide the special and non-printing characters in your document by clicking the ¶ tool on the **Standard** toolbar so that the document is numbered correctly.

* Place the insertion point where you want to insert the index.

* **Insert - Index and Tables**

* Activate the **Index** tab if you need to.

* Choose the **Type** of subentry:

  Indented   Subentries are indented in relation to main entries and are listed one above the other.

  Run-in   Entries are listed one after the other, and subentries are listed side-by-side, separated by semi-colons.

* Choose from the **Formats** and check the result in the **Print Preview** box.

* When possible, and if you need to, choose: **Right align page numbers**, **Columns**, **Tab leader** and **Language**.

* Click **OK**.

* If necessary, press [Alt][F9] to hide the code that corresponds to the index so that you can see its contents.

📄 *The styles used in an index, called Index 1, Index 2..., can be modified. As for the table of contents, make sure that your document is correctly numbered before adding an index.*

▪ Updating an index

* Click in the index.

  The grey background shows that it is active.

* Press [F9].

Below, you can see **Practice Exercise** 3.2. This exercise is made up of 7 steps. If you do not know how to complete one of the steps, go back to the lesson to refer to the corresponding title. When you have finished, check your work by reading the **Solution** on the next page.

Steps that are likely to be tested on the exam are marked with a 🪟 symbol. It is however recommended that you follow the whole exercise in order to gain a complete understanding of the lesson.

👉 Practice Exercise 3.2

To start working on exercise 3.2, you need to open *3-2 Getting around in Florida.doc* in the *MOUS Word 2000 Expert* folder.

1. Open the document outline in **Outline** view and apply the following styles to each heading as shown below:

Heading	Style to apply
DRIVING	Heading 1
Traffic	Heading 2
Signs	Heading 2
If you break down	Heading 2
TRANSPORT	Heading 1
By air	Heading 2
By road	Heading 2
Hire cars	Heading 3
Chauffeur-driven cars	Heading 3
Motorbikes	Heading 3
Coaches	Heading 3
By train	Heading 2

Return to Print Layout view.

2. Apply outline **Level 4** to the paragraphs with the **VL subheading** style (Conditions, Details, Hiring a car).

3. Show headings of **Level 3** and above.

   Move the **By air** heading to after the **By train** heading, to achieve the following result:

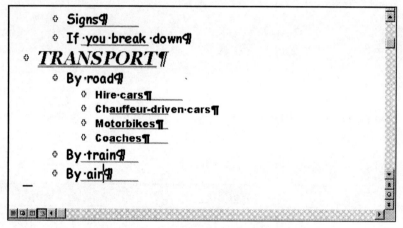

   Print the document outline and return to Print Layout view.

4. Insert a table of contents in the last paragraph of page 2. Use the **Formal** format and show headings up to level 4.

5. Apply the **Heading 2** style to the **American cars** heading (page 4) and the **VL subheading** style to the **Cost** and **Fuel** headings on page 6.
   Update the table of contents.

6. To continue exercise 3.2, you need now to open **3-2 Getting around in Florida 2.doc** in the **MOUS Word 2000 Expert** folder.

   To the right of the **Signs** heading (page 3), create the following index entry:
   Driving
     Signs

Create the following index entry to the right of **By road** (page 5):

Transport
    By road

To the right of **Motorbikes** (page 6), create this index entry:

Motorbike
    Hire

For each of these index entries, the page number is to be shown in the index.

Insert the index (below is an extract) at the end of the document (the other entries have already been created):

B	*M*
Breakdown 4	Motorbike
	Hire 6
C	Motoribike
	Travelling 6
Car	
Chauffeur driven 6	*P*
Cost 6	
Fuel 6	Petrol
Hire car conditions 5	Car 6
Hire car details 5	Plane 7
How to hire a car 5	
Cars	*R*
American cars 4	
Coach	Road
Travelling 6	Transport 5

7. Create this index entry to the right of **Motorbikes** (page 6):

Travelling
    Motorbike

Update the index.

If you want to put what you have learned into practice in a real document, you can work on the summary exercise 3 for the LONG DOCUMENTS section that you can find at the end of this book.

LONG DOCUMENTS
Exercise 3.2: Outlines and tables

It is often possible to perform a task in several different ways, but here only the quickest solution is presented. Go back to the lesson to see the other techniques that can be used.

 Solution to Exercise 3.2

1. Create the document outline in Outline view by first using **View - Outline**.
   To apply the styles shown in step 1 to the different headings:
   - click the heading in question (e.g.: DRIVING),
   - open the **Styles** drop-down list on the **Formatting** toolbar,
   - click the name of the style you want to apply (e.g.: Heading 1).

   To return to Print Layout view, use **View - Print Layout**.

2. To apply outline "Level 4" to paragraphs with the "VL subheading" style, use **Format - Style**.
   Select the **VL subheading** style in the **Styles** list then click **Modify**.
   Click the **Format** button and choose **Paragraph** in the list.
   Open the **Outline level** list and choose **Level 4**.
   Click **OK** twice, then **Close**.

3. To show headings of level 3 and above, use **View - Outline** then click the **3** button on the **Outlining** toolbar.

   Move the "By air" heading to after the "By train" heading by pointing to the cross before the text **By air** and dragging it to after the **By train** heading.

   To print the document outline, click the **4** button to show all the headings in the document then click 🖨.

   Return to Print Layout viewing using **View - Print Layout**.

⊞ 4. Insert the table of contents by clicking in the last paragraph on page 2, using **Insert - Index and Tables**, and activating the **Table of Contents** tab. Open the **Formats** list and choose **Formal**.
Type **4** in the **Show levels** box and click **OK**.

⊞ 5. To apply the "Heading 2" style to "American cars", click the heading, open the **Styles** list box, and choose **Heading 2**.

To apply the "VL subheading" style to "Cost", click the heading, open the **Styles** list box, and choose **VL subheading**.
To apply the "VL subheading" style to "Fuel", click the heading, open the **Styles** list box, and choose **VL subheading**.

Update the table of contents by clicking before **Driving** in the table of contents then pressing F9.
Activate the **Update entire table** option and click **OK**.

⊞ 6. To create an index entry to the right of "Signs", click at the end of this heading and press Alt Shift **X**.
Type **Driving** in the **Main entry** box and **Signs** in the **Subentry** box. Click **Mark** then **Close**.

To create an index entry to the right of "By road", click at the end of this heading and press Alt Shift **X**.
Type **Transport** in the **Main entry** box and **By road** in the **Subentry** box. Click **Mark** then **Close**.

To create an index entry to the right of "Motorbikes", click at the end of this heading and press Alt Shift **X**.
Type **Motorbike** in the **Main entry** box and **Hire** in the **Subentry** box. Click **Mark** then **Close**.

To insert the index, press Ctrl End to go to the end of the document, then click ¶ if necessary.
Activate **Insert - Index and Tables** and click the **Index** tab.
Open the **Formats** list and choose **Modern**.
Activate the **Right align page numbers** option, select the first style in the **Tab leader** list and click **OK**.

7. To create a second index entry to the right of "Motorbikes", click at the end of this heading and press `Alt` `Shift` **X**.

Type **Travelling** in the **Main entry** box and **Motorbike** in the **Subentry** box. Click **Mark** then **Close**.

To update the index, activate it then press `F9`.

LONG DOCUMENTS
Lesson 3.3: Master documents

1. Creating a master document 140

2. Using a master document 141

Practice Exercise 3.3 143

◨1 ▪ Creating a master document

A master document contains a group of documents (called sub-documents). You can use this technique to manage long documents by splitting them into smaller ones.

▪ Create a new document, using the same template as all the sub-documents.

▪ **View - Outline**

*Word displays the **Outlining** toolbar (you can move it if all the tools are not visible).*

▪ If necessary, click ⬚ to go to **Master Document** view.

▪ To insert a sub-document, click the ⬚ tool, select the document you want to insert, and click **Open**.

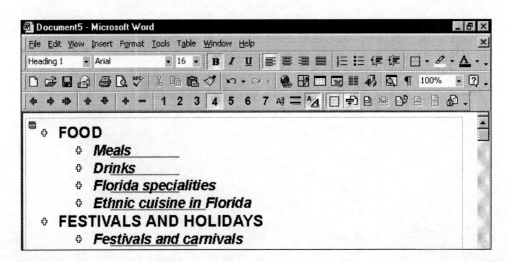

The outline of the sub-document appears in a grey frame.

▪ Save the master document and close it.

▦2 ▪ Using a master document

* Open the master document that contains the sub-documents.

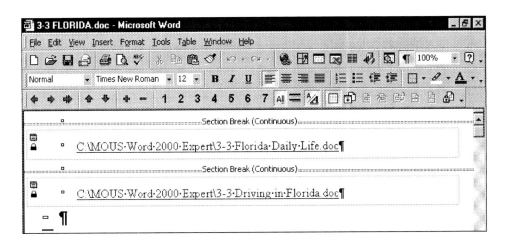

When you open a master document, it is collapsed. You can click the hyperlinks to open the sub-documents. If the non-printing characters are displayed, you will notice that the sub-documents are separated by section breaks.

* Click the [icon] tool to expand the sub-documents.

* Choose which headings you want to see using the tools on the **Outlining** toolbar.

* To open a sub-document, click its icon 🖿 in the top left corner of the frame, and, when you have finished, close the document to return to the master document.

If you do not close the sub-document, it is locked in the master document (a padlock appears under the 🖿 icon) and you will not be able to make changes to it.

LONG DOCUMENTS
Lesson 3.3: Master documents

- To lock a sub-document to prevent changes from being made, click in the sub-document then on the tool. To unlock, click again.

- To reorganise the contents of a master document, select the heading(s) in the sub-document that you want to move and click or or point to the cross next to the heading and drag it to its new position.

- To move heading, you can also use the and tools.

- To split a sub-document, place the insertion point where you want to cut the document and click .

In order for the tool to be available, the insertion point must be positioned right at the start of the paragraph.

- To merge sub-documents, select them then click .

In order for the tool to be available, no paragraph must be selected (not even a blank paragraph) outside the subdocument frames .

- To delete a sub-document, select the sub-document by clicking its icon then press .

The document is no longer part of the master document. You can still work with it as you would any document in Word.

- To insert or delete page or section breaks in a master document, you need to show the non-printing characters, and then proceed as you would in **Normal** or **Print Layout** view.

- To number the headings, pages, insert a table of contents, and index, create headers and footers..., do so as you would in any Word document.

- To print all the sub-documents, print the master document.

Below, you can see **Practice Exercise** 3.3. This exercise is made up of 2 steps. If you do not know how to complete one of the steps, go back to the lesson to refer to the corresponding title. When you have finished, check your work by reading the **Solution** on the next page.

All the steps in this exercise are likely to be tested in the exam.

☞ Practice Exercise 3.3

1. Create a master document, in which you must insert, in this order, the sub-documents **3-3 Daily Life in Florida.doc** and **3-3 Driving in Florida.doc** from the **MOUS Word 2000 Expert** folder.

   Save the master document under the name **3-3 FLORIDA.doc** in the **MOUS Word 2000 Expert** folder and close it.

2. Open the **3-3 FLORIDA.doc** master document and make the following changes:

   - delete the last paragraph marker (¶) in the master document.
   - expand the sub-documents to see their contents.
   - delete the **Section Break** at the top of the document.
   - show all headings of level 4 and above.
   - move the heading **Drinks** to after the heading **Ethnic cuisine in Florida**.
   - split the second sub-document at the **TRANSPORT** heading.
   - open the last sub-document to delete the picture on page 1, then close it, saving it in the **MOUS Word 2000 Expert** folder under the name **3-3 Getting around in Florida.doc**.
   - number the headings of the outline as shown below (a preset style has been applied to each heading).

LONG DOCUMENTS
Exercise 3.3: Master documents

```
✛  I-→FOOD¶
    ✛  A.·Meals¶
    ✛  B.·Florida·specialities¶
    ✛  C.·Ethnic·cuisine·in·Florida¶
    ✛  D.·Drinks¶
✛  II-·FESTIVALS·AND·HOLIDAYS¶
    ✛  A.·Festivals·and·carnivals¶
    ✛  B.·National·holidays¶
✛  III-  →    TO·SMOKE·OR·NOT·TO·SMOKE¶
✛  IV-  →    TIPS¶
```

- save the changes made to the master document.
- show the master document in print preview then print it.

If you want to put what you have learned into practice in a real document, you can work on the summary exercise 3 for the LONG DOCUMENTS section that you can find at the end of this book.

It is often possible to perform a task in several different ways, but here only the quickest solution is presented. Go back to the lesson to see the other techniques that can be used.

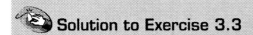

Solution to Exercise 3.3

1. To create a master document, click [icon] to create a new document then activate **View - Outline**.

   If necessary, activate the [icon] tool on the **Outlining** toolbar to go to **Master Document** view.

   Insert the first sub-document by clicking [icon], select the **MOUS Word 2000 Expert** folder and double-click the **3-3 Florida Daily Life.doc** document.

   Insert the second sub-document by clicking [icon], and double-clicking **3-3 Driving in Florida.doc** in the **MOUS Word 2000 Expert** folder.

   Save the master document by clicking [icon], select the **MOUS Word 2000 Expert** folder, type **3-3 FLORIDA.doc** in the **File name** box then click **Save**.

   Close the document using **File - Close**.

2. To open 3-3 FLORIDA.doc, click the [icon] tool, select the **MOUS Word 2000 Expert** folder and double-click **3-3 FLORIDA.doc**.

   If necessary, show the non-printing characters by clicking [icon].

   To delete the last paragraph marker, click it and press [Del].

   To expand the sub-documents, click [icon] on the **Outlining** toolbar.

LONG DOCUMENTS
Exercise 3.3: Master documents

To delete the **Section Break** at the top of the document, click it and press `Del`.

Show headings from level 4 and above by clicking **4** on the **Outlining** toolbar.

To move the "Drinks" heading to after "Ethnic cuisine in Florida", point to the cross that precedes **Drinks** and drag the heading to after **Ethnic cuisine in Florida**.

To split the second sub-document at TRANSPORT, place the insertion point before the **T** in the **TRANSPORT** heading and click [icon] on the **Outlining** toolbar.

Open this last sub-document by double-clicking the sub-document icon [icon]. Click the picture on the first page and press `Del`.
Close this document using **File - Close**. Click **Yes** and type **3-3 Getting around in Florida.doc** in the **File name** box. Choose the **MOUS Word 2000 Expert** folder in the **Save in** list and click **Save**.

To number the outline headings as shown in step 2, place the insertion point in any of the sub-documents, activate **Format - Bullets and Numbering**, **Outline Numbered** tab.
Select the third style on the second row and click **OK**.

Save the master document by clicking [icon].

See the print preview of the master document by clicking [icon] then click [icon] to print.

MAIL MERGE
Lesson 4.1: Forms

1. Creating a form.. 148

2. Inserting form fields... 149

3. Defining the properties of a text box form field.............. 149

4. Defining the properties of a drop-down form field 150

5. Defining the properties of a check box form field 151

6. Protecting a form.. 152

7. Using a form 153

Practice Exercise 4.1 154

MAIL MERGE
Lesson 4.1: Forms

1 ▪ Creating a form

A form is a document that contains unchanging text and spaces for filling in variable data. Example:

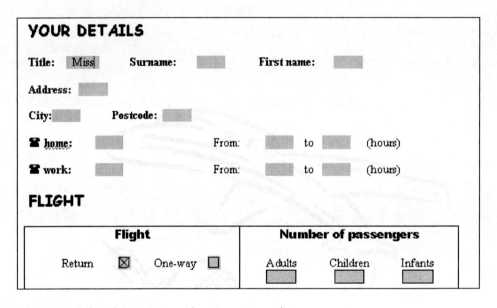

- Create or make changes to a document template.

- Enter the unchanging text.

- Wherever you want information to be filled in, insert a form field using the **Forms** toolbar (see below).

- When you have finished creating the form, protect it then save it.

2 ▪ Inserting form fields

*A **form field** can be a text box, a drop-down list or a check box.*

» Show the **Forms** toolbar using **View - Toolbars - Forms**.

» Place the insertion point where you want to insert the form field.

» Click [abl] to insert a text box field, [✓] for a check box or [▦] for a drop-down field.

The field appears as a grey box in the document.

» Define the properties of the field (see below).

 If the field codes are displayed, you will see the fields as follows: {FORMTEXT} for a text box, {FORMCHECKBOX} for a check box and {FORMDROPDOWN} for a drop-down list. To show or hide the field codes, press [Alt][F9].
These three types of form field can only be used if the document is protected as a form.

3 ▪ Defining the properties of a text box form field

» Click in the text field in question, and then click [▣] on the **Forms** toolbar.

» Decide on the **Type** of text box.

» Indicate any **Default text**, the **Maximum length** and the **Text format** of the text box, if necessary.

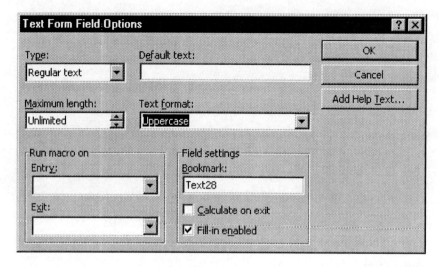

■ If you want a comment to appear on the status bar, click the **Add Help Text** button and type the text in the **Type your own** box then click **OK**.

■ Click **OK** to close the **Text Form Field Options** dialog box.

4 ▪ Defining the properties of a drop-down form field

■ Click in the drop-down list in question then on the [icon] tool on the **Forms** toolbar.

The insertion point is placed before the field.

■ For each item that is to appear in the list, enter the text in the **Drop-down item** box then click **Add**.

■ If you want to remove an item, select it in the **Items in drop-down list** box and click **Remove**.

■ If you need to, reorganise the list using the **Move** arrows.

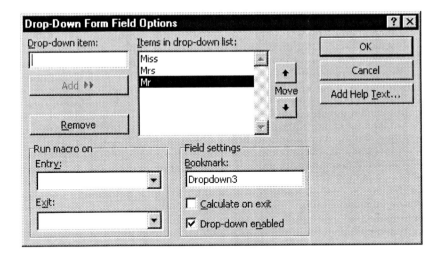

* If you want a comment to appear on the status bar, click the **Add Help Text** button and type the text in the **Type your own** box then click **OK**.

* Click **OK**.

The first item in the list is always displayed be default.

📖5 ▪ Defining the properties of a check box form field

* Click in the check box in question and click 📠 on the **Forms** toolbar.

The insertion point is placed before the check box.

* Define the properties of the check box using the options in the **Check box size** and **Default value** frames.

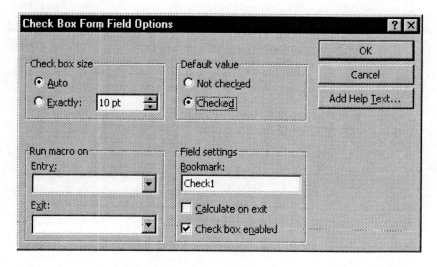

- If you want a comment to appear on the status bar, click the **Add Help Text** button and type the text in the **Type your own** box then click **OK**.

- Click **OK**.

▣6 ▪ Protecting a form

- Make sure you have finished creating the document.

- **Tools - Protect Document**

- Activate the **Forms** option.

- Enter a **Password**, if necessary, of a maximum of 15 characters.

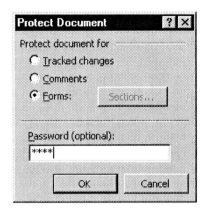

On the screen, the characters of a password are always replaced with asterisks (*). Pay careful attention to the case of the characters.

※ Click **OK**.

For security, you are asked to re-enter the password.

※ Type the password again then click **OK**.

📄 *To remove the protection, use **Tools - Unprotect Document** and type the password that protects the document. Be careful to respect the character case.*

 The 🔒 *tool allows you to protect/unprotect a document without entering a password.*

7 ▪ Using a form

※ Create a new document based on the form template.

The first field is selected and its help text (if there is any) is shown on the status bar. The fact that the document is protected as a form means that only the form fields can be accessed.

※ Move from field to field using ⇥ and ⇧⇥ and fill out the form.

MAIL MERGE
Exercise 4.1: Forms

Below, you can see **Practice Exercise** 4.1. This exercise is made up of 7 steps. If you do not know how to complete one of the steps, go back to the lesson to refer to the corresponding title. When you have finished, check your work by reading the **Solution** on the next page.

Steps that are likely to be tested on the exam are marked with a ▦ symbol. It is however recommended that you follow the whole exercise in order to gain a complete understanding of the lesson.

☞ Practice Exercise 4.1

In order to complete exercise 4.1, you will need to open the document template **4-1 Information sheet.dot,** *in the* **MOUS Templates** *folder, which is a subfolder of* **C:\Windows\Application Data\Microsoft\Templates.**

▦ 1. Change the document template by adding text as shown below:

If you can see the field codes, hide them.

▦ 2. Insert text box fields after the tab stops that follow the text **Surname**, **First name,** a drop-down list field after the tab stop that follows **Title**, and a check box field after the tab stop that follows **One-way** (in the first table). If you cannot see the non-printing characters, displaying them will facilitate these insertions. You can always hide them afterwards.

You should obtain the result below:

YOUR DETAILS

Title: ▢   **Surname:** ▢   **First name:** ▢

Address: ▢

City: ▢   **Postcode:** ▢

☎ **home:**   ▢   From: ▢ to ▢   (hours)

☎ **work:**   ▢   From: ▢ to ▢   (hours)

FLIGHT

Flight		Number of passengers		
Return ▢ One-way ▢		Adults ▢	Children ▢	Infants ▢

---

3. Define the properties of the text box fields that follow **Surname** and **Postcode** as follows:

   Surname   Regular text, unlimited maximum length, UPPERCASE formatting.

   Postcode   Regular text, maximum length 7 characters.

4. Define the properties of the drop-down list to the right of **Title** so that it contains the choices **Miss, Mrs** and **Mr**.

5. Change the properties of the check box to the right of **Return** so that it is active by default.

6. Protect the document as a form, using the password **form** (in lowercase). Save the changes you have made and close the form.

7. Use the **4-1 Information sheet.dot** template to fill out the form fields as shown below:

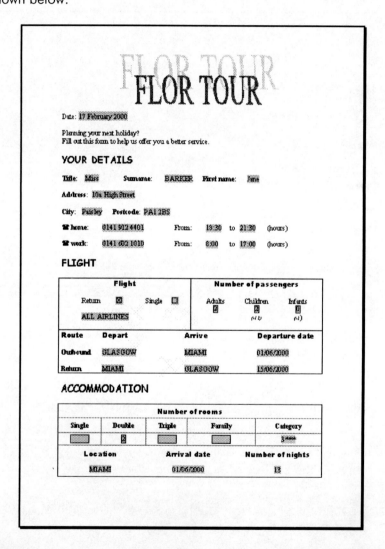

FLOR TOUR

Date: 17 February 2000

Planning your next holiday?
Fill out this form to help us offer you a better service.

YOUR DETAILS

Title: Miss   Surname: BARKER   First name: Jane

Address: 10a High Street

City: Paisley   Postcode: PA1 2BS

☎ home: 0141 912 4401   From: 18:30 to 21:30 (hours)

☎ work: 0141 602 1010   From: 8:00 to 17:00 (hours)

FLIGHT

Flight		Number of passengers		
Return ☒ Single ☐		Adults ☑	Children ☑ (r1)	Infants ☑ (r1)
ALL AIRLINES				

Route	Depart	Arrive	Departure date
Outbound	GLASGOW	MIAMI	01/06/2000
Return	MIAMI	GLASGOW	15/06/2000

ACCOMMODATION

Number of rooms				
Single	Double	Triple	Family	Category
☐	☑	☐	☐	3 stars

Location	Arrival date	Number of nights
MIAMI	01/06/2000	13

If you want to put what you have learned into practice in a real document, you can work on the summary exercise 4 for the MAIL MERGE section that you can find at the end of this book.

It is often possible to perform a task in several different ways, but here only the quickest solution is presented. Go back to the lesson to see the other techniques that can be used.

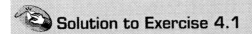
Solution to Exercise 4.1

1. To add the text shown in step 1 to the document template, click in the second paragraph after the text "Date" and type **Planning your next holiday?** then press ⏎. On the next line, type **Fill out this form to help us offer you a better service**.

   If you need to, hide the field codes by pressing ⌨Alt ⌨F9.

2. Before inserting the form fields after "Surname" and "First name", click the ⏎ tool, if necessary, to show the non-printing characters, then activate **View - Toolbars - Forms**. Place the insertion point after the tab stop (→) that follows the text **Surname** then click ⌨abl. Next, place the insertion point after the tab stop (→) that follows **First name** and click ⌨abl.

   To insert a drop-down list after "Title", place the insertion point after the tab stop (→) that follows the text **Title** and click ⌨.

   Insert the check box field after the tab stop (→) that follows the text "One-way" by placing the insertion point after the tab stop and clicking ⌨✓.

   To hide the non-printing characters, click the ⏎ tool.

MAIL MERGE
Exercise 4.1: Forms

3. To define the properties of the "Surname" text field, click it, then the ▦ button on the **Forms** toolbar.
   Open the **Text format** list, choose **Uppercase**, and click **OK**.

   Define the properties of the "Postcode" text field by clicking in the field, then on the ▦ tool on the **Forms** toolbar.
   In the **Maximum length** box, type 7, and then click **OK**.

4. To define the properties of the "Title" drop-down list, select the field then click ▦.
   Type **Miss** in the **Drop-down item** box then click **Add**. Type **Mrs** in the **Drop-down item** box then click **Add**. Type **Mr** in the **Drop-down item** box then click **Add**, then **OK**.

5. Define the properties of the "Return" check box field by selecting the field then clicking ▦.
   Activate the **Checked** option in the **Default value** frame.

6. To protect the form use **Tools - Protect Document**. Activate the **Forms** option.
   Type **form** in lowercase in the **Password** box, click **OK**, and re-type form (still in lowercase) then click **OK** again. Save the changes you have made by clicking ▦. Close the form by **File - Close**.

7. Use the 4-1 Information sheet.dot form template by using **File - New**, click the **MOUS Templates** tab then double-click the **4-1 Information sheet.dot** template.
   Move from field to field using ▦ and ▦ so that you can fill out the form as shown in step 7.
   Save this document if you like.

MAIL MERGE
Lesson 4.2: Mail Merge

1. Creating a main mail merge document 160

2. Creating a data file 162

3. Associating a data file to the main document 164

4. Inserting a field 164

5. Running the mail merge 165

6. Merging only certain records 166

7. Merging according to certain criteria 167

8. Managing the records in a data file 168

9. Sorting a data file 171

10. Making labels 172

Practice Exercise 4.2 174

Step-by-step creation of a mail merge

*The **mail merge** feature enables you to send large numbers of documents to a list of recipients, whose details are stored in a data file.*

* This feature requires the use of two files:

  - a **data file**, which contains the variable information,

  - a **main document**, which contains unchanging text.

* If necessary, create a data file. A data file is made up of **fields** and **records**. Example:

Surname	First name	Address	Town	Postcode
DANIELS	Alison	10 High Street	Paisley	PA1 2AE
START	Karen	12 Cannon Street	Salford	M3 6WA

Each line of information constitutes a record (here, there are two records). Each column is a field.

The records are numbered. The numbers correspond to the order in which they were entered, or to a sort order applied later.

* If necessary, create a main document (see 1.).

* Associate the data file to the main document (see 3.).

* Insert merge fields in the main document in the appropriate places (see 4.).

* Run the mail merge (see 5.).

1 ▪ Creating a main mail merge document

* Create a new document in which you need to enter the unchanging text, and apply the necessary formatting.

* **Tools - Mail Merge**

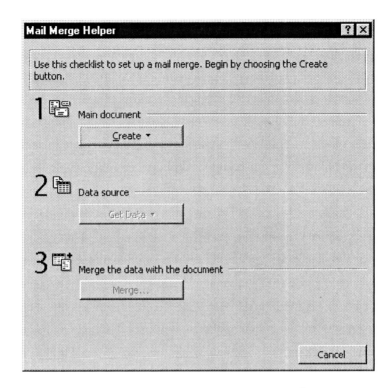

At the moment, you can only work in the **Main document** frame.

* Click the **Create** button and choose the **Form letters** option.

* Click the **Active window** option to indicate that the main document is in the active window.

  If this is not the case, click the **New main document** button to create a new document.

  The second frame, **Data source**, becomes active.

* If you want to work in your main document, click **Close**. If not, keep this dialog box open.

  If you close the **Mail Merge Helper** *dialog box, a new toolbar appears - the* **Mail Merge** *toolbar.*

▣2 ▪ Creating a data file

※ Open the main document and activate **Tools - Mail Merge**.

※ Click the **Get Data** button and choose to **Create Data Source**.

*In the **Field names in header row** list, Word suggests a list of common field names.*

※ Click each field name you do not want to use then click **Remove Field Name**.

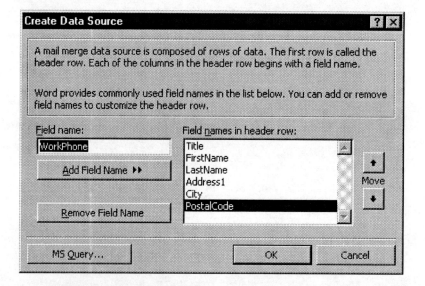

If you want to create custom field names, delete the name in the **Field name** box, type the new field name then press the **Add Field Name** button.

The custom fields are added to the end of the list.

It is useful if the fields appear in the same order as that in which you are going to enter the data.

» If you need to move a field, select it in the **Field names in header row** list and use the **Move** arrows.

» Once you have finished creating the structure of your data file, click **OK**.

» Enter the name of the file and choose, if necessary, the folder in which you want to store it.

Word detects that the file contains no records and asks if you want to change the source data.

» Click the **Edit Data Source** button.

A data form appears.

» For each record:

- type the data and press 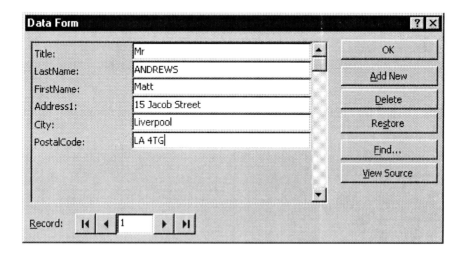 to go to the next field or ⇧ to return to the previous field.

- after the last field, press ↵ to create a new record, or do nothing.

You can also press ↵ to go to the next text box.

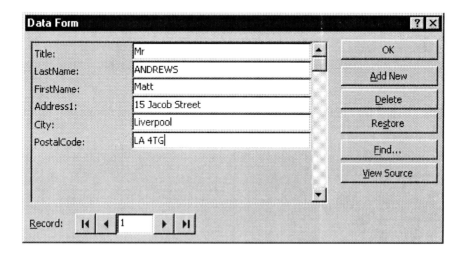

* Once you have finished entering the records, you need to save the changes made to the data file. Do this by clicking the **View Source** button, then the 🖫 tool.

* Close the data file using **File - Close**.

You return to the main document.

🪟3 ▪ Associating a data file to the main document

* Open the main document and use **Tools - Mail Merge**.

* Click the **Get Data** button.

* If you want to **Create Source Data**, click the corresponding button. See the section above for instructions on how create a data file.

* If your data file already exists, click **Open Data Source**, double-click the file in question then click **Edit Main Document**.

🪟4 ▪ Inserting a field

The data file needs to be associated with the main document.

* Place the insertion point where the field contents are to appear.

* Click the **Insert Merge Field** button on the **Mail Merge** toolbar.

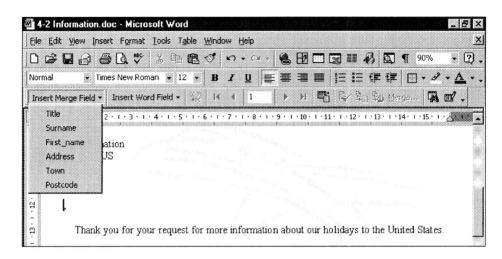

All the fields in the data file are shown.

» Click the field you want to insert.

📠5 ▪ **Running the mail merge**

This is the moment when you merge the main document and the data file.

» If necessary, open the main document.

» Click:

 to print the mail merge.

 to create form letters for each record in a new document.

» If you merge to a new document, print and save this document, if necessary, then close it.

📄 *The* 🔲 *tool allows you to check the merge before running it.*

🗐6 ▪ Merging only certain records

* Activate the main document.

* **Tools - Mail Merge** or 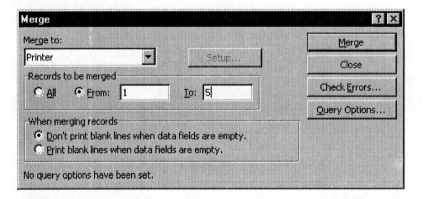 on the **Mail Merge** toolbar.

* Click the **Merge** button.

* Choose whether or not to print the mail merge in the **Merge to** list.

* In the **Records to be merged** frame, enter the number of the first and last records you want to merge.

* Click **Merge**.

* If you have chosen to merge to the **Printer**, select the necessary print options and click **OK**.

* If you have chosen to merge to a **New document**, print and save this document, if you want to, then close it.

📄 *If you want to merge again later, you might want to change the options in the **Merge** dialog box's **Records to be merged** frame.*

▥7 ▪ **Merging according to certain criteria**

- ▨ Activate the main document.

- ▨ **Tools - Mail Merge** or on the **Mail Merge** toolbar.

- ▨ Click the **Merge** button.

- ▨ Make sure that **All** is the active option in the **Records to be merged** frame. If it is not, activate it.

- ▨ Click the **Query Options** button.

- ▨ If necessary, activate the **Filter Records** tab.

- ▨ For each condition:

  - select the field name in the **Field** list,

  - use the **Comparison** list to select the comparison operator,

  - type the **Compare to** value in the box with the same name,

  - if you do not want to set any more conditions, click **OK**,

  - if you have further conditions, choose the combination operator: **And** if the conditions are all to be met, **Or** if one or the other of the conditions is to be met.

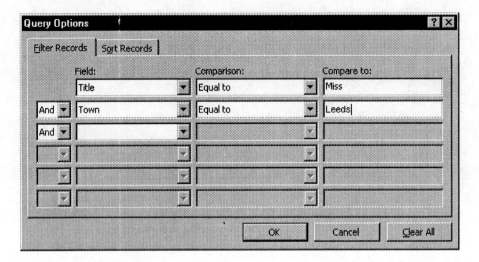

* Click **OK** to confirm.

* Merge by clicking **Merge**, or click **Close** to put the merge on stand-by.

📄 *The conditions you have set are saved in the main document.*

👆 *To delete the conditions you have set, click the **Clear All** button in the **Query Options** dialog box.*

8 ▪ Managing the records in a data file

Accessing the data form

* Click the 📝 tool on the **Mail Merge** toolbar.

The data form appears and you can see the first record.

*Notice the number 1 in the **Record** box.*

* Use the buttons at the bottom of the form to scroll through the records.

Adding a record

* Go to the data form.

* Click the **Add New** button.

  *An empty data form with the number of the current **Record** appears.*

* Enter the new record as you did the others.

Finding a record

* Go to the data form.

* Show the first record.

* Click the **Find** button.

* In the **Find what** box, type the value you want to find.

* In the **In field** drop-down list, choose the name of the field that contains this value.

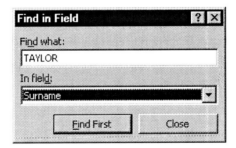

* Start searching by clicking the **Find First** button as many times as is necessary to reach the appropriate record.

* Click **Close** when you have finished searching.

Deleting a record

* Go to the data form.
* Show the record you want to delete.
* Click **Delete**.

 Be very careful with this command: deletion is instant.

Modifying a record

* Go to the data form.
* Show the record you want to modify.
* Make your changes.
* If you make a mistake, click the **Restore** button to return to the old data.
* When you have finished making changes, click **OK** to close the data form.

To change the structure of a data file, open the data file as a document (the records are shown in a table). Make the necessary changes then save the document.

☐9 ▪ Sorting a data file

▪ Activate the main document.

▪ **Tools - Mail Merge** or 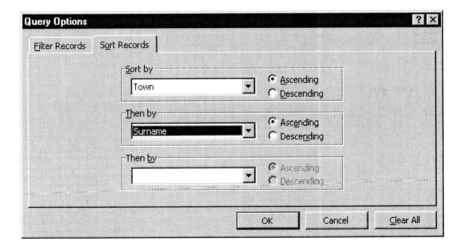 on the **Mail Merge** toolbar.

▪ Click the **Merge** button then the **Query Options** button.

▪ If necessary, activate the **Sort Records** tab.

A data file can be sorted by up to three criteria.

▪ Open the **Sort by** list, click the name of the field by which you want to sort, and choose whether the data should be sorted in **Ascending** or **Descending** order.

▪ If several records are likely to have the same value chosen in the **Sort by** list, specify a second criterion in the first **Then by** list.

▪ Click **OK**.
▪ Click **Close** twice.

10 ▪ Making labels

- Create a new document.

- **Tools - Mail Merge**

- Click the **Create** button in the **Main document** frame.

- Choose **Mailing Labels**.

- Click **Active window**.

- Click the **Get Data** button in the **Data source** frame then choose to either **Create** or **Open Source Data**.

  Word analyses the first record and indicates that you must Set Up Main Document.

- Click the **Set Up Main Document** button.

- Use the **Label Options** dialog box, and the **Details** button (if necessary), to define the characteristics of your labels.

- Click **OK**.

- Insert each field in the label using the **Insert Merge Field** list.

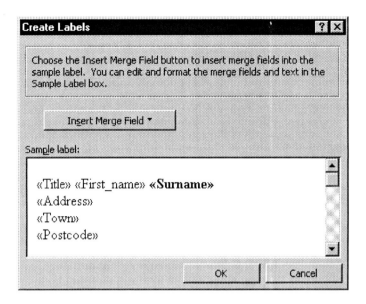

» Format the contents of the **Sample label** frame. To do this by selecting the field(s) in question, right-clicking the selection, and choosing the **Font** or **Paragraph** option.

» Once you are happy with your label, click **OK**.

» Click **Close**.

A sheet of labels is created.

Print the labels in the same way as you run any mail merge. The labels document is simply a special type of main document.

Below, you can see **Practice Exercise** 4.2. This exercise is made up of 10 steps. If you do not know how to complete one of the steps, go back to the lesson to refer to the corresponding title. When you have finished, check your work by reading the **Solution** on the next page.

Steps that are likely to be tested on the exam are marked with a ▦ symbol. It is however recommended that you follow the whole exercise in order to gain a complete understanding of the lesson.

☞ **Practice Exercise 4.2**

In order to complete exercise 4.2, you need to open *4-2 Information.doc* in the *MOUS Word 2000 Expert* folder.

▦ 1. Carry out the actions necessary to make **4-2 Information.doc** the main document in a mail merge. The main document should be shown on screen after you have made the changes.

▦ 2. Using the main document **4-2 Information.doc**, create the data file shown below. Save this data file under the name **4-2 Addresses.doc** in the **MOUS Word 2000 Expert** folder. The fields should appear in the order in which you enter the data.

Title	FirstName	LastName	Address1	City	PostalCode
Mr	ANDREWS	Matt	15 Jacob Street	Liverpool	L8 4TG
Mrs	BARCLAY	Mary	41 Royston Way	Slough	SL1 6ES
Mr	BOND	Julian	8 Stonefield Park	Maidenhead	SL6 6ES
Miss	BOWEN	Carol	58 Westminster Road	Birmingham	B20 3LJ
Mr	BROWN	Jack	6 Stephens Grove	Morecombe	LA3 3HX

3. Associate the data file **4-2 Customers.doc** (in the **MOUS Word 2000 Expert** folder) with the main document **4-2 Information.doc**.

4. Insert the merge fields into the main document **4-2 Information.doc** as shown below:

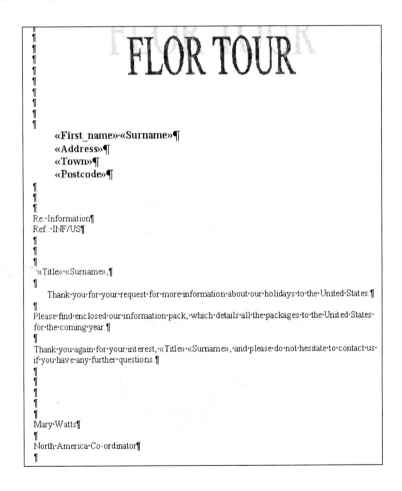

5. Merge to a new document, check the result in the first letter the close the document without saving it.

6. Run a merge which will print letters for only the first **five** records in the data file.

7. Run a merge which will only print letters for customers with the title **Miss**, living in **Leeds**.

8. Go to the data form and make the following changes:

- add this record: **Mrs BARKER, Sheila, 17 Newbattle Road, Dalkeith, EH22 3LJ**.

- find the record for **Mr TAYLOR** and delete it.

- Mrs JOHNSON's address has changed to **23 Milehouse Park**. Find her record and change this information.

9. Sort the data file by **Town** then by **Surname**. Both these fields should be sorted in ascending order.

10. Create labels for the customers in the **4-2 Customers.doc** data file like the one shown below. The reference number of the labels is **2160 Mini-Address**, the surname should appear in bold type on each label and a left indent of **1 cm** should be applied to the whole address:

«Title» «First_name» **«Surname»**
«Address»
«Town»
«Postcode»

Run a mail merge to a new document to see the result.

If you want to put what you have learned into practice in a real document, you can work on the summary exercise 4 for the MAIL MERGE section that you can find at the end of this book.

It is often possible to perform a task in several different ways, but here only the quickest solution is presented. Go back to the lesson to see the other techniques that can be used.

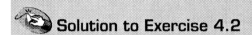

Solution to Exercise 4.2

1. To make 4-2 Information.doc the main document for a mail merge, activate **Tools - Mail Merge**.
   Click the **Create** button and choose **Form Letters**.
   Click the **Active Window** button then **Close** to return to the main document.

2. To create the data file shown in step 2, activate **Tools - Mail Merge**, click **Get Data**, then choose **Create Data Source**.
   Remove the **JobTitle, Company, Address2, State, Country, HomePhone** and **WorkPhone** fields: select each field in the **Field names in header row** list and click the **Remove Field Name**.

   Click the **LastName** field and click the ⬆ button once.
   Click **OK**.
   Type **4-2 Addresses.doc** in the **File name** box, select **MOUS Word 2000 Expert** folder then click **Save**.
   Click the **Edit Data Source** button and enter the records shown in the table in step 2, using ⇥ to go to the next field and ⇧⇥ to return to the previous field. Press ↵ to create a new record.

   Click **View Source** then click 🖫.
   Close the **4-2 Address.doc** data file by **File - Close**.

MAIL MERGE
Exercise 4.2: Mail Merge

▦ 3. To associate the data file 4-2 Customers.doc to the main document 4-2 Information.doc, activate **Tools - Mail Merge**.
Click the **Get Data** button and choose **Open Data Source**.
Select the file **4-2 Customers.doc** in the **MOUS Word 2000 Expert** folder then click **Open**.
Click the **Edit Main Document** button.

▦ 4. Follow the instructions below for each merge field to be inserted into the main document **4-2 Information.doc**:

- place the insertion point where the field contents are to appear.

- click the **Insert Merge Field** button on the **Mail Merge** toolbar.

- click the name of the field you want to insert.

▦ 5. Click the ⬚ button to merge the data to a new document, and scroll down to look at the result in the first letter.

Close the document using **File - Close** then click **No** when Word asks you if you want to save the changes.

▦ 6. To run a mail merge that will print only the first five records in the data file, first click the ⬚ tool on the **Mail Merge** toolbar and then click **Merge**.
Open the **Merge to** list and choose **Printer**.
Type **1** in the **From** box and **5** in the **To** box then click **Merge**.
Click **OK** to print.

▦ 7. In order to run a mail merge concerning only the « Miss » customers from Leeds, activate **Tools - Mail Merge** and click the **Merge** button.
In the **Merge to** list, choose **Printer**, activate the **All** option in the **Records to merge** frame then click the **Query Options** button.

Fill out the **Query Options** dialog box as shown below:

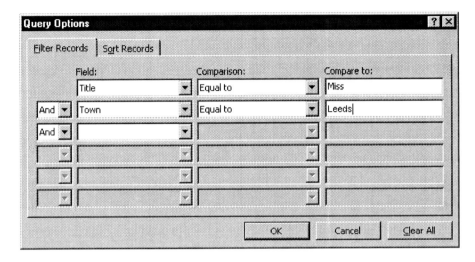

Click **OK** then **Merge**.

Click **OK** to print.

8. Access the data form by clicking the ![tool icon] tool on the **Mail Merge** toolbar.

Add the record for Mrs BARKER by clicking **Add New** and filling out the form as shown below.

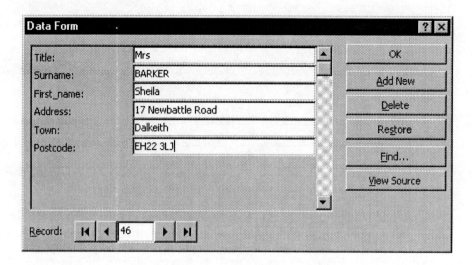

To find the record for Mr TAYLOR, click the ⏮ button to go to the first record, then **Find**.

Type **TAYLOR** in the **Find what** box, and choose **Surname** in the **In field** list.

Click the **Find First** button then click **Close**.

Delete the record for Mr TAYLOR by clicking **Delete**.

To change the record for Mrs JOHNSON, find her record by clicking **Find**, type **JOHNSON** in the **Find what** box and choose **Surname** in the **In field** list. Click **Find First** then **Close**.

Select the contents of the **Address** field, press ⌈Del⌋ then type **23 Milehouse Park**.

Click **OK** to confirm these changes.

⊞ 9. Sort the data file according to Town then Surname by first activating **Tools - Mail Merge**, and clicking the **Merge** button.

Click the **Query Options** button, then the **Sort Records** tab.

Fill out the dialog box as shown below:

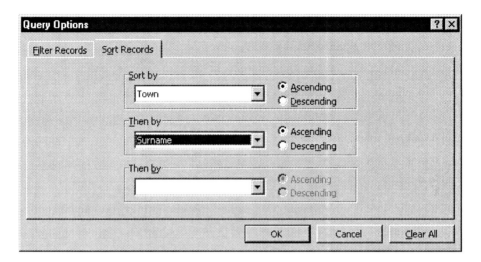

Click **OK** then **Close** twice.

📁10. In order to create labels for the customers in the 4-2 Customers.doc data file, click the ▢ tool to create a new document then activate **Tools - Mail Merge**.

Click the **Create** button, choose the **Mailing Labels** option then click the **Active Window** button.

Click the **Get Data** button then choose **Open Data Source**.

Select the file **4-2 Customers.doc** in the **MOUS Word 2000 Expert** folder and click **Open**.

Click the **Set Up Main Document** button.

Select **2160 Mini-Address** in the **Product number** list then click **OK**.

Press ⏎ to leave a space at the top of the label and insert the fields into the label as shown in step 10, using the list on the **Insert Merge Field** button.

So that the surname on each label appears in bold, select the «Surname» field, right-click the selection, and choose **Font**.

In the **Font style** list, choose **Bold** then click **OK**.

To apply a left indent of 1 cm to the whole label, select all the lines, right-click the selection and click **Paragraph**.
Type **1** in the **Left** box in the **Indentation** frame then click **OK**.

Now that the label is finished, click **OK** then **Close**.

Run the mail merge to a new document by clicking the tool on the **Mail Merge** toolbar.

ADVANCED FUNCTIONS
Lesson 5.1: Macros

1. Creating a macro.. 184

2. Running a macro 185

3. Editing a macro 186

4. Deleting a macro... 187

5. Managing a macro project.. 188

Practice Exercise 5.1 190

1 ▪ Creating a macro

A macro is a series of commands that are saved as one command, allowing you to automate work in Word. Macros are written in the Visual Basic programming language. They are stored in a document or document template.

▪ If the macro is to be recorded in a particular document or template, open the document (if it is a template, you can open a document based on the template). If there are no open documents, the macro will be recorded in the global template (Normal.dot).

▪ **Tools - Macro - Record New Macro**

▪ Type the **Macro name**.

▪ Indicate the document or document template in which you want to record the macro using the **Store macro in** drop-down list.

*You can record macros in the global template (**All documents (Normal.dot)**), the active document or the active document's template.*

▪ Add a **Description** if you want to.

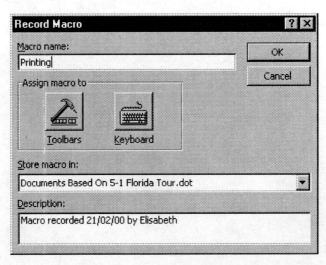

» To be able to run a macro quickly, you can assign a button and/or a shortcut key by clicking the following buttons:

Toolbars   to insert the macro in the appropriate toolbar, creating a button.

Keyboard   to assign a keyboard shortcut to the macro.

» Click **OK**.

*The macros toolbar appears (its name is **Stop Recording**, but **Stop** is all that fits on the title bar) and the letters **REC** are visible on the status bar.*

» Carry out all the actions you want to record in the macro.

» If you want to do something that you do not want to record in the macro, pause the recording by clicking the ⏸ button on the **Stop** toolbar. To re-start recording click this button again.

» Once you have completed all the actions, click the ⏹ button on the **Stop Recording** toolbar.

*The letters **REC** appear grey on the toolbar.*

2 ▪ Running a macro

» **Tools - Macro - Macros** or Alt F8

*The **Macros** dialog box opens and contains a list of all available macros.*

» If necessary, open the **Macros in** drop-down list to select the document or template that contains the macro you want to run.

» In the **Macro name** list, choose the macro you want to run.

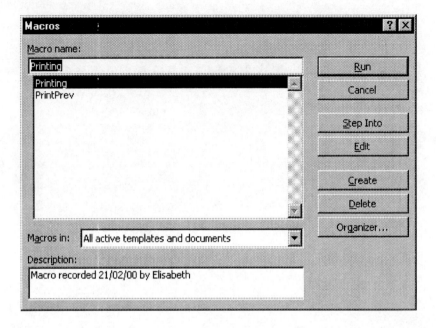

* Click **Run**.

> If you have assigned a button or a shortcut key to the macro, click this button or use the shortcut key to run the macro.

3 • Editing a macro

* **Tools - Macro - Macros** or Alt F8
* Select the macro in the **Macro name** list.
* Click **Edit**.

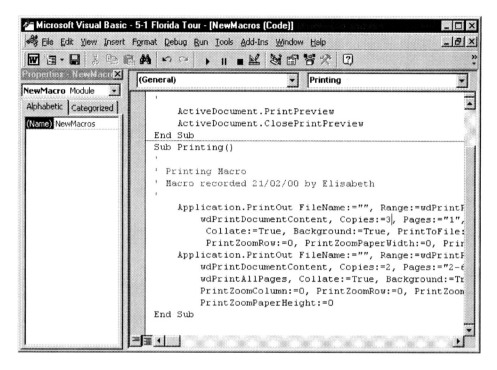

The Visual Basic application window opens. The macro is shown as it has been saved, in Visual Basic.

» Make the necessary changes.

» Leave Microsoft Visual Basic by **File - Close and Return to Microsoft Word** or Alt **Q**.

⊞4 ▪ Deleting a macro

» **Tools - Macro - Macros** or Alt F8

» Click the macro you want to delete in **Macro name**.

» Click **Delete**.

» Confirm by clicking **Yes**.

187

▪ Click **Close**.

🖱5 ▪ Managing a macro project

*The different macros that you save in a template or document are regrouped in a macro called a **Macro project**, called **NewMacros** by default.*

Going to the Organizer dialog box

▪ Open the document or template that contains the macro project you want to change.

▪ **Tools - Macro - Macros** or Alt F8

▪ Click the **Organizer** button.

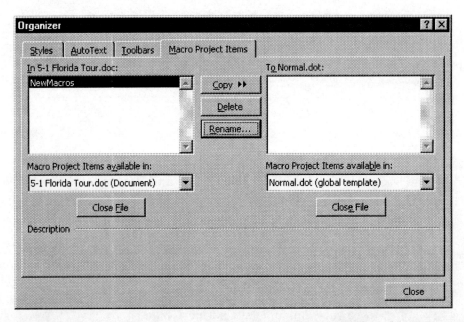

*The **Organizer** dialog box opens, and the **Macro Project Items** tab is active. In the list on the left, Word lists the macro projects in the active document, and on the right the macro projects in the global template (Normal.dot).*

* Open one of the **Macro Project Items available in** drop-down lists to see the macro projects in the current template or document.

* To see a template other than **Normal.dot**, click the **Close File** button under the list on the right then click the **Open File** button that replaces it, and select the template you want.

Copying a macro project

* If necessary, select the source and destination templates. To do this, click the **Close File** button then open the **Macro Project Items available in** drop-down list.

* Select the macro project(s) you want to copy in one of the lists.

* Click **Copy.**

  The macro project is copied into the other template instantly.

* Click **Close**.

   To copy a single macro, edit it and use the features in Visual Basic.

Rename/delete a macro project

* If necessary, select the source template in one of the **Macro Project Items available in** lists.

* Select the macro project you want to rename.

* To rename the macro project, click **Rename**, enter the new name and click **OK** then **Close**.

* To delete the macro project, click **Delete**, and confirm your choice by clicking **OK**. Close the dialog box by clicking **Close**.

ADVANCED FUNCTIONS
Exercise 5.1: Macros

Below, you can see **Practice Exercise** 5.1. This exercise is made up of 5 steps. If you do not know how to complete one of the steps, go back to the lesson to refer to the corresponding title. When you have finished, check your work by reading the **Solution** on the next page.

All the steps in this exercise are likely to be tested in the exam.

☞ Practice Exercise 5.1

*In order to complete exercise 5.1, you need to open **5-1 Florida Tour.doc** in the **MOUS Word 2000 Expert** folder.*

1. Create a macro that will print one copy of the first page of the document and two copies of all the other pages. Call this macro **Printing** and save it in the **5-1 Florida Tour.dot** template.

2. Run the macro you have just recorded.

3. Edit the **Printing** macro so that three copies of the first page are printed.

4. Delete the macro called **PrintPrev**.

5. Rename the macro project called "NewMacros" with the name **FloridaMacro**.

If you want to put what you have learned into practice in a real document, you can work on the summary exercise 5 for the ADVANCED FUNCTIONS section that you can find at the end of this book.

It is often possible to perform a task in several different ways, but here only the quickest solution is presented. Go back to the lesson to see the other techniques that can be used.

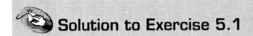

Solution to Exercise 5.1

1. To create a macro that will print one copy of the first page of the document and two copies of the remaining pages, run **Tools - Macro - Record New Macro**.
   In the **Macro name** box, type **Printing**. In the **Store macro in** list, choose **Documents Based On 5-1 Florida Tour.dot** then click **OK**.

   Carry out the following actions:
   File - Print; activate the **Pages** option and type **1** in the text box then click **OK**.
   File - Print; activate the **Pages** option and type **2-6** in the text box; type **2** in the **Copies** box then click **OK**.

   Click the ■ button on the **Stop** toolbar to stop recording the macro.

2. Run the macro you have just recorded by activating **Tools - Macro - Macros**.
   Make sure that **Printing** is selected then click **Run**.

3. To change the "Printing" macro to print three copies of the first page of the document, use **Tools - Macro - Macros**. Make sure that the **Printing** macro is selected then click the **Edit** button.
   In the Microsoft Visual Basic window, change the **Copies:= 1** instruction to **Copies:= 3**.
   Leave the Microsoft Visual Basic window by **File - Close and Return to Microsoft Word**.

4. Delete the "PrintPrev" macro by activating **Tools - Macro - Macros**. Click the **PrintPrev** macro then the **Delete** button.
Confirm by clicking **Yes** then **Close**.

5. Rename the "NewMacros" macro project to "FloridaMacro", activate **Tools - Macro - Macros** then click **Organizer**.
Select the **NewMacros** macro project and click the **Rename** button. Type **FloridaMacro** then click **OK** followed by **Close**.

ADVANCED FUNCTIONS
Lesson 5.2: Toolbars

1. Customising a toolbar 194

2. Creating a custom toolbar.. 197

Practice Exercise 5.2 199

1 ▪ Customising a toolbar

Open the Customize dialog box

✳ You need to be in the document or template in question.

✳ If necessary, show the custom toolbar.

✳ **View - Toolbars - Customize**

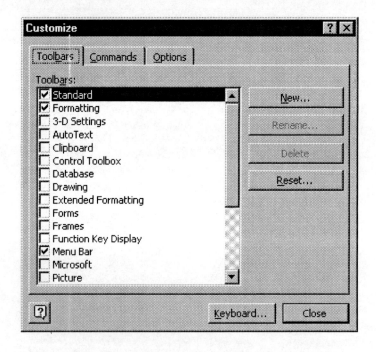

📄 *You can also open this dialog box using **Tools - Customize**.*

Deleting a tool

- Open the **Customize** dialog box.
- Click the tool you want to delete and drag it off the bar.

  As soon as release the mouse button, the tool disappears.

Adding a tool

- Open the **Customize** dialog box.
- Activate the **Commands** tab.
- In the **Categories** list, select the category of the tool you want to add.
- In the **Commands** frame, click the line that corresponds to the tool you want to add.

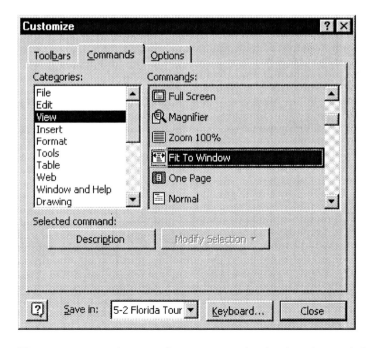

*The **Description** button allows you to check what the tool does.*

* Drag the tool from the dialog box to the destination toolbar in the Microsoft Word window.

* You can use the **Modify Selection** button to choose what the button should display.

Customising the appearance of a tool

* Open the **Customize** dialog box.

* If necessary, activate the **Commands** tab.

* Click the tool you want to customise on the toolbar.

* Click the **Modify Selection** button under the **Commands** tab.

* Use the different options in this menu to make changes to the appearance of the tool.

Leave the customisation of toolbars

* In the **Save in** list, choose the document or template concerned.

* Click **Close**.

 *You can also add or remove buttons from a toolbar by clicking the black triangle at the right of most toolbars then clicking the **Add or Remove Buttons** option.*

*As long as you have not saved the template or document, you can return to the original toolbars. Use **Tools - Customize**, activate the **Toolbars** tab, choose the toolbar in question then click the **Restore** button and confirm with **OK**.*

2 ▪ Creating a custom toolbar

- Open the template or document in which you want to use the toolbar.
- **View - Toolbars - Customize**
- Activate the **Toolbars** tab.
- Click the **New** button.
- Enter the **Toolbar name**.
- In the **Make toolbar available to** list, choose the template or document concerned.

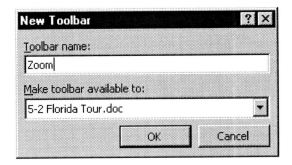

- Click **OK**.

  The name of the new toolbar appears at the end of the ***Toolbars*** *list in the* ***Customize*** *dialog box. The new bar appears in the Word window as a floating toolbar.*

- Add the appropriate tools using the options in the **Commands** tab.

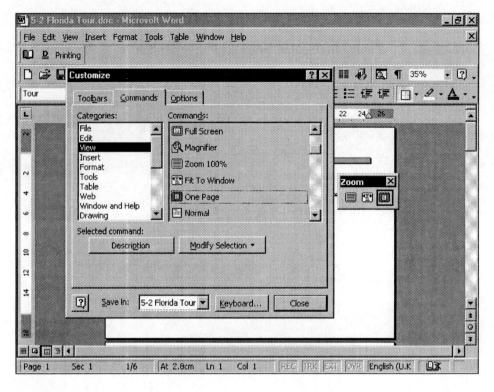

※ Click **Close**.

※ Dock the toolbar by double-clicking its title bar.

Below, you can see **Practice Exercise** 5.2. This exercise is made up of 2 steps. If you do not know how to complete one of the steps, go back to the lesson to refer to the corresponding title. When you have finished, check your work by reading the **Solution** on the next page.

Both the steps in this exercise are likely to be tested in the exam.

Practice Exercise 5.2

*In order to complete exercise 5.2, you will need to open **5-2 Florida Tour.doc** in the **MOUS Word 2000 Expert** folder.*

1. Show the custom toolbar **Florida** then make the following changes:
   - delete the [□] tool.
   - change the text "Project.NewMacros.Printing" to **Printing**.

2. Create a toolbar called **Zoom** and save it in **5-2 Florida Tour.doc**. Add the following buttons: [□], [□] and [□], which can be found in the **View** category.

If you want to put what you have learned into practice in a real document, you can work on the summary exercise 5 for the ADVANCED FUNCTIONS section that you can find at the end of this book.

It is often possible to perform a task in several different ways, but here only the quickest solution is presented. Go back to the lesson to see the other techniques that can be used.

 Solution to Exercise 5.2

1. To show the custom toolbar "Florida", use **View - Toolbars - Florida**. To customise this toolbar, use **View - Toolbars - Customize**.

   Delete the ▣ tool by clicking it on the **Florida** toolbar then dragging it off the bar.

   To change the text "Project.NewMacros.Printing" to "Printing", activate the **Commands** tab if necessary.
   Click the button in question on the **Florida** toolbar then click **Modify Selection**.
   In the **Name** text box, type **Printing** then press ↵.

   Close the **Customize** dialog box by clicking **Close**.

2. To create the Zoom toolbar in 5-2 Florida Tour.doc, activate **View - Toolbars - Customize**. Click **New** under **Toolbars** tab.
   Type **Zoom** in the **Toolbar name** box and select **5-2 Florida Tour.doc** in the **Make toolbar available to** drop-down list.
   Click **OK**.

   Add the tools ▤, ▦ and ▣ by activating the **Commands** tab and selecting **View** in the **Categories** list.
   In the **Commands** list, click the **Zoom 100%** command and drag it to the **Zoom** toolbar. Do the same thing for the commands **Fit To Window** and **One Page**.
   Click **Close** to leave the **Customize** dialog box.

ADVANCED FUNCTIONS
Lesson 5.3: Workgroups

1. Managing comments 202

2. Tracking changes made by several users to
   the same document 204

3. Protecting a document 208

4. Associating a password with a document.................................... 210

5. Creating several versions of a document.................................... 211

6. Managing document versions 211

7. Defining the default workgroup templates folder............................ 214

8. Navigating between HTML documents 216

Practice exercise 5.3 218

▦1 ▪ **Managing comments**

Creating a comment

This feature allows you to associate comments with sections of text. These comments can be particularly useful in a document that is available to several users.

▪ Select the text that is to carry the comment.

▪ **Insert - Comment**

▪ Enter the comment text in the pane that opens at the bottom of the screen.

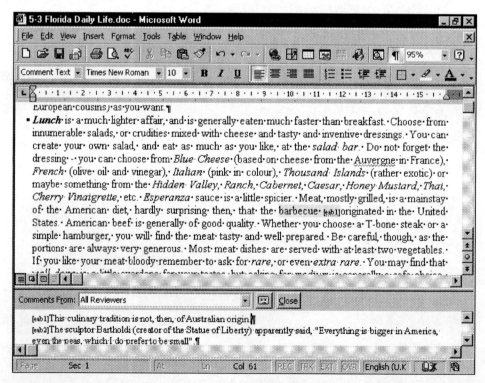

*If your computer is fitted with a sound card, you can use the button to the left of the **Close** button to record an audio comment.*

» Click **Close**.

*The insertion point of the comment is highlighted in pale yellow. The comment reference is shown underlined between square brackets if the **Hidden text** option is active in the **Options** dialog box (**Tools - Options, View** tab), or if you are displaying non-printing characters.*

Viewing a comment

» To see a comment in a ScreenTip, point the mouse pointer at the yellow-highlighted text.

» To see the comments in the comments pane, use **View - Comments**, or double-click a comment reference (e.g.: [eab2]).

» To go to the next or previous comment, click ⬛ or ⬛ on the **Reviewing** toolbar.

» To see the comments of a particular user, show the comment pane, open the **Comments from** list and click the name of the user in question.

▤ *You can also use the **Select Browse Object** button.*

Editing a comment

» Click the yellow-highlighted text associated with the comment you want to edit.

» **View - Comments** or ⬛ on the **Reviewing** toolbar.

You can also double-click the comment reference.

» Make changes to the comment in the comments pane then click **Close**.

Deleting a comment

▪ Click the yellow-highlighted text associated with the comment you want to delete.

▪ Click the 🔲 tool on the **Reviewing** toolbar.

You can also select the appropriate comment reference and press 🔲 Del .

Printing comments

▪ To print comments at the same time as the document, use **File - Print** then click the **Options** button.
Activate the **Comments** option in the **Include with document** frame then click **OK**.
If necessary, define the print options and click **OK**.

▪ To print only the comments, use **File - Print**. In the **Print what** list, choose **Comments** then click **OK**.

▣2 ▪ Tracking changes made by several users to the same document

When several people want to work on the same document you can make copies of the document. These copies can be merged at a later date to create a single document.

Making a document available to several users

Before you make any copies of a document, you must set it up so that you can track the changes.

▪ Open the document that you want to make available to several users.

▪ **Tools - Track Changes - Highlight Changes**

▪ Activate the **Track changes while editing** option.

» Leave the **Highlight changes on screen** option active if you want to see revision marks on the screen (such as inserted text shown underlined and deleted text shown with a line through it).

» Leave the **Highlight changes in printed document** option active if you want to see the revision marks when you print the document.

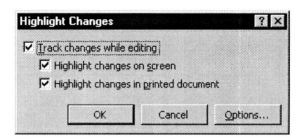

» Click **Options** if you want to change the marks that Word uses to highlight different changes then click **OK** to confirm your choices.

» Click **OK**.

» Now you can make the document available to other users by copying it onto the network into one or more folders accessible to other users. To do this, use **File - Save As**, or make the copies using **Windows Explorer**.

If you wish, give each copy a different name.

*To start tracking changes, you can also double-click the grey text **TRK** on the status bar.*

ADVANCED FUNCTIONS
Lesson 5.3: Workgroups

Merging documents

By merging documents, you can regroup, in the original document, all the changes (insertions, text deletions, formatting changes...) and comments made in the document copies by different users. This does depend on you having activated the tracking options in the original document before making copies for other users.

- Open the original document in which you want to group the changes.

- For each copy you want to merge:

- use **Tools - Merge Documents**,

- select the folder that contains the document you want to merge then double-click the document in question, or select it and click **Open**.

- if necessary, click **OK** to confirm the message that appears.

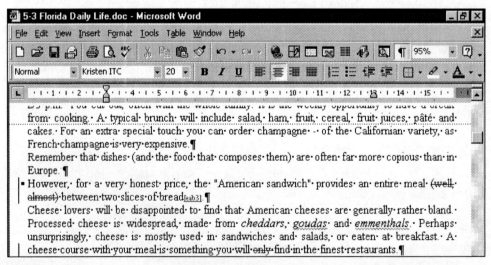

The changes and comments made by different users are visible. Different colours are used for comments and changes.

MOUS
Word 2000 Expert

Accepting or rejecting changes

The changes you can see after merging the document can either be rejected or incorporated into the document.

- Open the document in which the documents have been merged and place the insertion point wherever you want to start reviewing the document.

- **Tools - Track Changes - Accept or Reject Changes**

- Before choosing to accept or reject the changes, you can decide what you want to see in the document by selecting one of the options in the **View** frame:

Changes with highlighting   to see all the changes made to the document.

Changes without highlighting   to see the document as it would be if you accepted all the changes.

Original   to see the original document as it would be if you refused all the changes.

- If you want to accept or reject the changes one by one, use the **Find** buttons to move from change to change and use **Accept** and **Reject** to make your choices.

Whichever view you chose previously, clicking Accept or Reject will activate ***Changes with highlighting.***

- If you want to accept or reject all the changes all at once, click **Accept All** or **Reject All**, then **Yes** to confirm.

  *The **Undo** button allows you to cancel the last action.*

  *In the **Changes** frame, you can see the name of the user who made the change and the date and time it was made.*

- When you reach the end of the document, Word might ask you to start checking at the beginning of the document. Click **Cancel**.

- Click the **Close** button to close the **Accept or Reject Changes** dialog box.

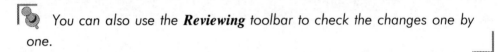 You can also use the ***Reviewing*** toolbar to check the changes one by one.

3 ▪ Protecting a document

Word will only allow you to protect certain items in a document.

- Open the document concerned.

- **Tools - Protect Document**

- Click one of the options in the **Protect document for** frame:

Tracked changes	The contents of the document can be changed, but all the changes made to the document will be highlighted so that they ·can be found easily. The tracking changes feature is activated and you cannot deactivate it. You cannot accept or reject any changes made to the document.
Comments	The contents of the document cannot be changed, and only comments can be added.
Forms	Users of a form can only access the form fields; the rest of the document is protected from changes. When a form contains several sections, the **Sections** button allows you to choose which sections are to be protected.

❋ If necessary, enter a **Password** (of a maximum 15 characters) in the corresponding text box.

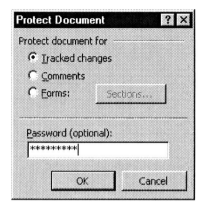

The characters entered are replaced with asterisks. Pay careful attention to the case, as Word is case-sensitive.

❋ Click **OK**.

For security, Word asks you to enter the password a second time.

❋ Enter the **Password** again then click **OK**.

❋ To remove the protection from a document, use **Tools - Unprotect Document**, enter the **Password** if necessary, and then click **OK**.

🗐4 ▪ **Associating a password with a document**

You can restrict access to a document by using a password.

▪ Open the document concerned.

▪ **Tools - Options - Save** tab

▪ If you want to control the opening of the document, type a password in the **Password to open** text box.

▪ Activate the **Read-only recommended** option if you want Word to display a message recommending the document be opened in read-only mode after the password has been entered.

▪ If you want to prevent changes being made, enter a password in the **Password to modify** text box.

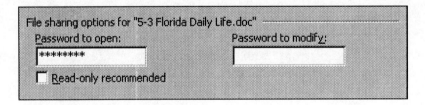

You cannot see the password as you type: the characters are replaced by asterisks (*). Be careful as to the case of the characters, Word is case-sensitive.

▪ Click **OK**.

▪ Type the **Password** again in the corresponding text box to confirm then click **OK**.

▪ Click the 🖫 tool to save the password.

*To remove a password associated with a document, delete the asterisks in the corresponding text box in the **Options** dialog box (**Tools - Options, Save** tab).*

⌸5 ▪ Creating several versions of a document

A version captures the document at a precise moment without creating a new file. The different versions are saved in the document itself, saving disk space.

▪ Open the document concerned.

▪ **File - Versions**

▪ Click the **Save Now** button.

▪ Type a comment.

▪ Click **OK**.

 *To create a version every time you close the document, activate the **Automatically save a version on close** option in the **Versions** dialog box (**File - Versions**).*

⌸6 ▪ Managing document versions

Opening a version

▪ Open the document concerned.

▪ **File - Versions**

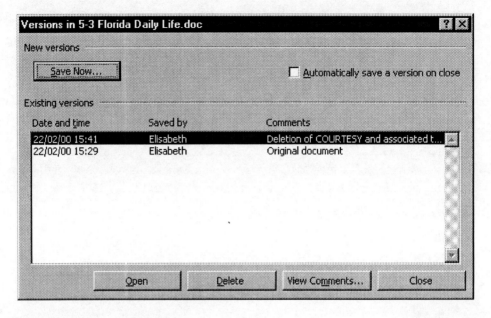

* Click the version you want to see.

* Click **Open** or double-click the name of the version.

📄 *To save a version as a file, open it then use **File - Save As**.*

Deleting a version

* Open the document concerned.

* **File - Versions**

* Select the version you want to delete.

* Click **Delete**.

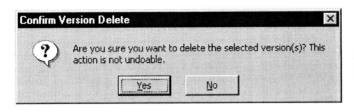

A confirmation message appears.

✳ Click **Yes**.

Viewing the comments in a version

✳ Open the document concerned.

✳ **File - Versions**

✳ Select the version whose comments you want to view.

✳ Click the **View Comments** button.

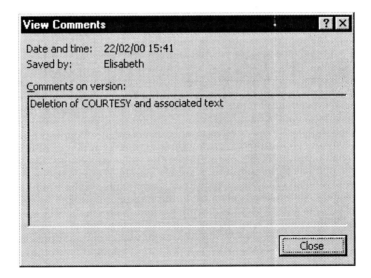

✳ After consulting the comments, click **Close**.

7 ▪ Defining the default workgroup templates folder

By default, your custom templates (User templates) are stored in the Templates folder (C:\Windows\Application Data\Microsoft\Templates) or in a subfolder of Templates. They can only be used by you are they are stored on your hard drive (C:\).

If you want to create templates that are to be used by several different users (Workgroup templates), you need to save these templates on the network in a folder that can be accessed by the users concerned. You also need to define the default workgroup templates folder.

▪ **Tools - Options - File Locations** tab

▪ In the **File types** list, click the **Workgroup templates** choice.

*By default, there is no **Location** associated with this choice.*

▪ Click the **Modify** button.

*A dialog box that looks like the **Open** and **Save As** dialog boxes appears.*

▪ If the folder exists already, go to the network and double-click the folder in question.

▪ If the folder does not exist, go to the network and the place where the folder is to be stored then click the tool. Type the **Name** of the folder in the corresponding box and click **OK**.

▪ Click **OK** to close the **Modify Location** dialog box.

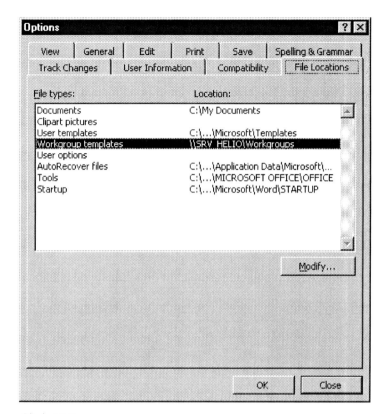

The folder's path appears on the **Workgroup templates** line.

* Click **OK**.

 *When you save a template, the user templates folder (C:\Windows\Application Data\Microsoft\Templates) is proposed by default in the **Save As** dialog box. To save the template in the Workgroup templates folder, select this folder in the **Save in** list in the **Save As** dialog box.*

*Templates saved in the Workgroup templates folder are visible in the **General** tab in the **New** dialog box (**File - New**).*

8 • Navigating between HTML documents

Retrieving an HTML page in Word

When a Web page created in Word is open in Internet Explorer 5, you can activate Word in order to save the Web page on your disk.

▪ Open the **Internet Explorer 5** browser; type the address of the Web page in the **Address** text box, and press ⏎.

▪ **File - Edit with Microsoft Word for Windows**

The Web page appears in Microsoft Word.

▪ Activate **File - Save As** to save the Web page on your disk.

▪ Close the HTML document using **File - Close**.

Going from Word to Internet Explorer

This feature allows you to go from Microsoft Word to your browser and back again, using a hyperlink. When an HTML file open in Word contains a hyperlink to another HTML file, if you click this link, the HTML file opens in your browser. Once in the browser, you can easily return to the original document in Word.

▪ Open the HTML file concerned in Word and, if one does not already exist, create a hyperlink to another HTML file.

Remember that you can create a hyperlink using **Insert - Hyperlink** (Ctrl **K**).

▪ Activate the hyperlink by clicking it.

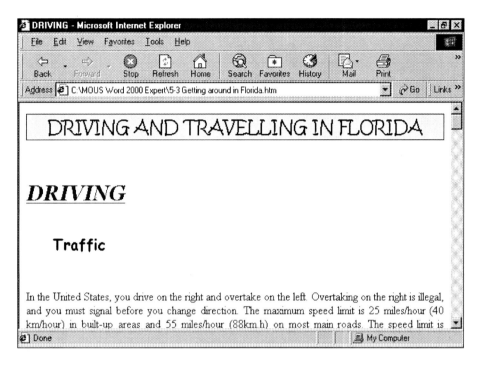

The HTML file opens in your browser.

■ To return to the original document in Word, click ⬅ Back .

The browser window closes.

Below, you can see **Practice Exercise** 5.3. This exercise is made up of 8 steps. If you do not know how to complete one of the steps, go back to the lesson to refer to the corresponding title. When you have finished, check your work by reading the **Solution** on the next page.

All the steps in this exercise are likely to be tested in the exam.

☞ Practice Exercise 5.3

In order to complete exercise 5.3, you will need to open **5-3 Florida Daily Life.doc** *in the* **MOUS Word 2000 Expert** *folder.*

1. For the text **barbecue** (page 1), create the comment **This culinary tradition is not, then, of Australian origin**.
   Change the comment associated with **Tallahassee** so that **106 West...** reads **107 West Gaines Street**.
   Delete the comment associated with **far more copious** (page 2).

2. Turn on Word's change-tracking feature then merge the active document (**5-3 Florida Daily Life**) with **5-3 Florida Daily Life (copy).doc**, which is in the **MOUS Word 2000 Expert** folder, and in which some changes have been made (insertion of a comment and deletion of text). Review the changes and accept them all except for the comment associated with the text **increases**.

3. Protect the revision marks and the use of change-tracking in the document, and use the password **flochange** (in lowercase).

4. Set the password **dailyflo** (in lowercase), which will be required before the document can be opened.

5. Delete the heading **COURTESY** (page 6) and the associated text (up to **as soon as you are introduced**). Create a version of the document with the associated comment **Deletion of COURTESY and associated text**.

6. Open the first version of the document. The comment for this version is **Original document**. Close this version then maximise the **5-3 Florida Daily Life.doc** window.

7. Define the default workgroup templates folder. If necessary, create this folder. Choose any name and location on the network you wish.

8. In Microsoft Word, open the HTML file **5-3 Florida Daily Life.htm**, which is in the **MOUS Word 2000 Expert** folder. Open the file about travelling in Florida using the hyperlink at the end of the document.
Finish by returning to **5-3 Florida Daily Life.htm** in Microsoft Word.

If you want to put what you have learned into practice in a real document, you can work on the summary exercise 5 for the ADVANCED FUNCTIONS section that you can find at the end of this book.

It is often possible to perform a task in several different ways, but here only the quickest solution is presented. Go back to the lesson to see the other techniques that can be used.

 Solution to Exercise 5.3

1. Create a comment associated with the text "barbecue" by selecting this text and using **Insert - Comment**.
   Type **This culinary tradition is not, then, of Australian origin** in the comments pane at the bottom of the screen then click **Close**.

   To change the comment associated with "Tallahassee" (page 4), click this text then **View - Comments**.
   Select the text **106**, press ⌷Del⌷ then type **107**.
   Click **Close**.

   Delete the comment associated with "far more copious" (page 2) by selecting the comment reference that follows the text **far more copious** and pressing ⌷Del⌷.

2. To turn on change-tracking, activate **Tools - Track Changes - Highlight Changes**. Activate the **Track changes while editing** option and click **OK**.

   To merge the active document (5-3 Florida Daily Life.doc) with 5-3 Florida Daily Life (copy).doc, activate **Tools - Merge Documents**.
   If necessary, select the **MOUS Word 2000 Expert** folder then double-click **5-3 Florida Daily Life (copy).doc**. If necessary, click **OK** to confirm the message that Word displays.

   Accept all the changes except the comment associated with the text "increases" by first pressing ⌷Ctrl⌷⌷↖⌷ to send the insertion point to the beginning of the document. Use **Tools - Track Changes - Accept or Reject Changes**.

Click the ⇨ Find button then **Reject** button. **Accept** the next two changes. When Word reaches the end of the document, click **Cancel** then **Close**.

3. To protect the revision marks in the document, use **Tools - Protect Document**, and leave the **Tracked Changes** option active.
Type the password **flochange** (in lower case) in the corresponding box then click **OK**.
Type the password again in the **Reenter password** box and click **OK**.

4. Control the opening of the document with the password "dailyflo" (in lowercase): activate **Tools - Options** then click the **Save** tab.
Type **dailyflo** in the **Password to open** text box and click **OK**.
Re-type the password in the **Reenter password** then click **OK**.

Save the document by clicking 💾.

5. Delete the heading "COURTESY" (page 6) and the associated text by selecting this text and pressing Del.

Create a version of the document by activating **File - Versions**. Click the **Save Now** button and type **Deletion of COURTESY and associated text** in the **Comments on version** text box then click **OK**

6. Open the first version of the document by activating **File - Versions**. Double-click the version with the comment **Original document**.

Close this version's window by clicking the ☒ button in the top right corner of the window.

Maximise the window of **5-3 Florida Daily Life.doc** by clicking the ▣ button in the top right corner of the document window.

7. To define the default workgroup templates folder, run **Tools - Options** and click the **File Locations** tab.
   In the **File types** list, click the **Workgroup templates** choice then click **Modify**.
   Go to the network and select the folder (or create it), then click **OK**.
   Click **OK** to close the **Options** dialog box.

8. To open, in Microsoft Word, the HTML file 5-3 Florida Daily Life.htm, click the ⬚ tool, and double-click **5-3 Florida Daily Life.htm** in the **MOUS Word 2000 Expert** folder.

   To open the HTML file about travelling in Florida, press ⟦Ctrl⟧⟦End⟧ to go the end of the document then click the **GETTING AROUND IN FLORIDA** hyperlink.

   Return to the **5-3 Florida Daily Life.htm** file in Word by clicking the ⟦← Back⟧ button.

SUMMARY EXERCISES

Summary 1   DOCUMENT CONTENTS 224

Summary 2   DOCUMENT PRESENTATION 227

Summary 3   LONG DOCUMENTS 228

Summary 4   MAIL MERGE 230

Summary 5   ADVANCED FUNCTIONS 232

SUMMARY EXERCISES

Open **Summary 1.doc** in the **Summary** folder of the **MOUS Word 2000 Expert** folder.

Sort the paragraphs that begin **THE THIRD MAN, THE ITALIAN JOB** and **THE COMMITMENTS** in ascending order.

In these three paragraphs, replace text with Bold and Italic formating with Blue characters in Bold and Italic, and with the Emboss Effect.

Sort the list showing the dates of the first showings in ascending order according to the date then the film name.

In the table on page 2, calculate the total audience numbers for each week.

Using the data in this table, insert a chart that represents the audiences for each showing, per week, and change the chart to obtain the result below:

Audience numbers for January:

Week	First showing	Second showing	Third showing	Fourth showing	Total number of receipts
Week 1	35	30	28	30	123
Week 2	36	32	45	38	151
Week 3	40	48	26	30	144
Week 4	42	46	25	48	161
Week 5	38	35	28	30	131

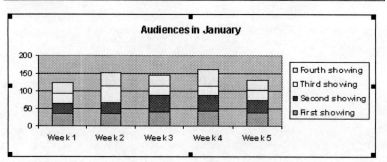

To obtain the chart shown above, you need to inverse the data series, change the chart type, add the title **Audiences in January** then resize the chart.

Under the text **Audience numbers for February**, embed the **films.xls** worksheet from the **Summary** folder in the **MOUS Word 2000 Expert** folder.

Under this table, create a chart by importing the data from the **February** worksheet of the **films.xls** workbook in the **Summary** folder on the **MOUS Word 2000 Expert** folder. This chart should represent the audience numbers for each showing per week for the month of February. You should obtain the result below:

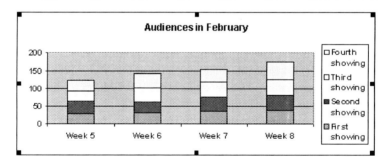

Audience numbers for February:

Week	First showing	Second showing	Third showing	Fourth showing	Total number of receipts
Week 5	30	35	28	30	123
Week 6	31	33	38	40	142
Week 7	35	40	42	37	154
Week 8	37	42	47	48	174

To obtain this chart, you need to inverse the data series, remove the last column (called **Total number of receipts**) from the datasheet, change the chart type, add the title **Audiences in February**, and resize the chart object.

On the third page of the document, reduce the height of the object with the title **THE ADVENTURES OF ROBIN HOOD**.

Under the paragraph **directed by Michael Curtiz...**, insert the picture called **Robin.tif** from the **Summary** folder in the **MOUS Word 2000 Expert** folder.

Change the picture's text wrapping, size, and position (if necessary) in order to obtain the result shown below:

The solution to this exercise is called **Solution 1.doc**.

Open the **Summary 2.doc** document in the **Summary** folder of the **MOUS Word 2000 Expert** folder.

Apply the background colour **Light turquoise** to the paragraph **You have decided that you want a dog**.

Apply a border of a double blue line to both pages of the document.

Insert the picture **Dog.bmp** from the **Summary** folder in the **MOUS Word 2000 Expert** folder as a watermark. You will need to change the picture's text wrapping, increase its size by approximately three times and position it in the centre of the page. Remember to activate the watermark setting.

On the first page of the document, insert the text **CHOOSING A DOG** as a horizontally centred header. The watermark inserted previously should still appear on page 1.

Use the formatting applied to the **THE CHOICES** paragraph to create a style called **POINT**.
Apply this style to the paragraphs: **DOES SIZE MAKE A DIFFERENCE?**, **WILL YOUR DOG HAVE A SPECIFIC PURPOSE?**, **WHAT IS YOUR ACTIVITY LEVEL?**, **HOW MUCH SPACE DO YOU HAVE?** and **DO YOU WANT A PEDIGREE OR A MONGREL?**
Change this style to use the font **Baskerville Old Face**, size **11**.
Delete the **SUBHEADING** style.

Change the columns so that they both have a width of **8 cm**.

Prevent the break between the paragraph: **WILL YOUR DOG HAVE A SPECIFIC PURPOSE?**, and the following paragraph.

The solution to this exercise is called **Solution 2.doc**.

Open **Summary 3.doc** in the **Summary** folder of the **MOUS Word 2000 Expert** folder.

Go to the **HenryVIII** bookmark. Delete this bookmark.

At the end of the paragraph about the **Cleveland Bay**, insert the footnote: **This breed is very popular as a police horse the world over**.
Change the appearance of the footnotes so that they are numbered 1, 2, 3... and not lettered a, b, c...

Make an outline of the document using its custom styles. To do this, apply outline level 1 to the style **MAIN HEADING**, level 2 to **PRIMARY HEADING** and level 3 to **SUBHEADING**.

At the beginning of the document, under the paragraph **TABLE OF CONTENTS**, insert the contents using the **Distinctive** format.

Complete the index entries by creating an index entry after the text **The true origins of the Shire**. The main entry is **Draught horse**, the subentry **Shire**.

Under the paragraph **INDEX** at the end of the document, insert an index using the **Modern** style.

The solution to this exercise is called **Solution 3A.doc**.

Create a master document and insert the subdocuments **Summary 3-1.doc** and **Summary 3-2.doc** from the **Summary** folder in the **MOUS Word 2000 Expert** folder.
Save this master document as **Cumbria.doc** in the **Summary** folder of the **MOUS Word 2000 Expert** folder.
Go to **Print Layout** view and insert the text **CUMBRIA** on the first page (above the section break). Format this text as you please.

Return to **Outline** view and collapse the subdocuments so that you can delete the last paragraph in the document (which is empty).

Expand the master document then number the headings using the **1, 1.1, 1.1.1** format.

Print a plan of the master document, then of the entire master document.

The solution to this exercise is called **Solution 3B.doc**.

Create the form below:

```
┌─────────────────────────────────────────────────┐
│  INFORMATION ABOUT ACCOMMODATION TO RENT          │
│                                                   │
│  Type:              One-room ▪                    │
│  Surface area:            sq ft.                  │
│  Monthly rent:                                    │
│                                                   │
│  Conditions:                                      │
│  ─────────────────────────────────────────────   │
│  Public transport close by:    □                  │
│  Amenities close by:           □                  │
│  Animals permitted:            ☒                  │
│                                                   │
│  Particular requirements:                         │
└─────────────────────────────────────────────────┘
```

The items to be included in the drop-down list are: **One-room, One-bed, Two-bed, Bungalow, Semi** and **Detached**.
The text field for the surface area is of **Number** type.

The monthly rent is a **Number** field with a currency format.

The check box opposite the animals point is checked by default.

Remember that documents that are forms are protected as such.

The solution to this exercise is called **Solution 4.dot** and can be found in the **MOUS Templates** folder.

Open the **Summary 4-1.doc** document in the **Summary** folder in the **MOUS Word 2000 Expert** folder.

Make this the main document for a mail merge and associate the data file **Summary 4-2.doc**. This last document contains the branch addresses, to whom the mail merge is destined. The form letter should look like the one shown below:

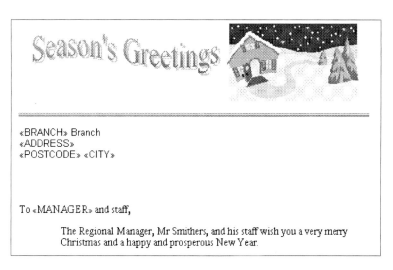

Make the following changes to the **Summary 4-2.doc** data file using the data form:

- The BRAID HILL branch has moved. The address has changed from "3 Memorial Drive" to **7 Main Street**.

- A new branch has been opened. Its details are: **MARKET ST., Miss Adams, 2 Market Street, FERN GROVE, 4120**.

- The BLACKFORD branch (in Herston) has been closed. Delete the appropriate record.

The solution to the main document is called **Solution 4A.doc** and the solution to the data file is called **Solution 4B.doc**.

Open the **Summary 5.doc** document in the **Summary** folder in the **MOUS Word 2000 Expert** folder.

Create a macro which will set two tab stops (at 5 and 12 cm) with a tab leader in the paragraphs that give the dates and times of film showings.
Call this macro **Tabs** and save it in the template associated with the active document (**Summary 5.dot**).
Associate a button on the **Summary 5: formatting** toolbar with this macro. The button should show the text **Tabs**.

Run this macro on the paragraphs that show the date and times of film showings.

On the **Summary 5: formatting** toolbar, delete the 📂 (open document) tool.

Create a version with the comment **Intermediate version**. Delete the version called **First version**.

Insert a comment that reads **Subject to change** for the word **APRIL**.

Use the password **MOUS** (in uppercase) to protect the active document from changes.

The solution to this exercise is called **Solution 5.doc** (password MOUS).

MICROSOFT Word 2000 Expert				
Table of Objectives 田				
Tasks	**Lessons**	**Pages**	**Exercises**	**Pages**
Working with paragraphs				
Apply paragraph and section shading	Lesson 2.1 Title 1	74	Exercise 2.1 Point 1	84
Use text flow options (Windows/Orphans options and keeping lines together)	Lesson 2.1 Title 4	78	Exercise 2.1 Point 4	84
Sort lists, paragraphs, tables	Lesson 1.1 Title 1	12	Exercise 1.1 Point 1	20
	Lesson 1.2 Title 1	24	Exercise 1.2 Title 1	40
Working with documents				
Create and modify page borders	Lesson 2.1 Title 2	74	Exercise 2.1 Point 2	84
Format first page differently than subsequent pages	Lesson 2.1 Title 6	81	Exercise 2.1 Point 6	85
Use bookmarks	Lesson 3.1 Title 5	115	Exercise 3.1 Point 5	119
Create and edit styles	Lesson 2.2 Titles 1 and 3	90 and 95	Exercise 2.2 Points 1 and 3	104
Create watermarks	Lesson 2.1 Title 5	80	Exercise 2.1 Point 5	84
Use find and replace with formats, special characters and non-printing elements	Lesson 1.1 Titles 2 and 3	13 and 14	Exercise 1.1 Points 2 and 3	20
Balance column length (using column breaks appropriately)	Lesson 2.1 Title 3	75	Exercise 2.1 Point 3	84

TABLE OF OBJECTIVES

Tasks	Lessons	Pages	Exercises	Pages
Create or revise footnotes and endnotes	Lesson 3.1 Titles 1, 3 and 4	110 and 113	Exercise 3.1 Points 1, 3 and 4	118 and 119
Work with master documents and subdocuments	Lesson 3.3 Titles 1 and 2	140 and 141	Exercise 3.3 Points 1 and 2	143
Create and modify a table of contents	Lesson 3.2 Titles 4 and 5	128 and 129	Exercise 3.2 Points 4 and 5	134
Create cross-reference	Lesson 3.1 Title 6	116	Exercise 3.1 Point 6	119
Create and modify an index	Lesson 3.2 Titles 6 and 7	130 and 132	Exercise 3.2 Points 6 and 7	134 and 135
Using tables				
Embed worksheets in a table	Lesson 1.2 Titles 6	32	Exercise 1.2 Point 6	41
Perform calculations in a table	Lesson 1.2 Titles 2 and 3	27 and 28	Exercise 1.2 Points 2 and 3	40
Link Excel data as a table	Lesson 1.2 Title 7	36	Exercise 1.2 Point 7	42
Modify worksheets in a table	Lesson 1.2 Title 8	37	Exercise 1.2 Point 8	42
Working with pictures and charts				
Add bitmapped graphics	Lesson 1.4 Title 1	62	Exercise 1.4 Point 1	69
Delete and position graphics	Lesson 1.4 Titles 2, 3 and 6	63 and 67	Exercise 1.4 Points 2, 3 and 6	69 and 70
Create and modify charts	Lesson 1.3 Titles 1 and 3	48 and 53	Exercise 1.3 Points 1 and 3	57 and 58

Tasks	Lessons	Pages	Exercises	Pages
Import data into charts	Lesson 1.3 Title 2	51	Exercise 1.3 Point 2	58
Using mail merge				
Create main document	Lesson 4.2 Title 1	160	Exercise 4.2 Point 1	174
Create data source	Lesson 4.2 Title 2	162	Exercise 4.2 Point 2	174
Sort records to be merged	Lesson 4.2 Title 9	171	Exercise 4.2 Point 9	176
Merge main document and data source	Lesson 4.2 Titles 5, 6 and 7	165 to 167	Exercise 4.2 Points 5, 6 and 7	175 and 176
Generate labels	Lesson 4.2 Title 10	172	Exercise 4.2 Point 10	176
Merge a document using alternate data sources	Lesson 4.2 Title 3	164	Exercise 4.2 Point 3	175
Using advanced features				
Insert a field	Lesson 4.1 Tiltle 2	149	Exercise 4.1 Point 2	154
	Lesson 4.2 Title 4	164	Exercise 4.2 Point 4	175
Create, apply and edit macros	Lesson 5.1 Titles 1, 2 and 3	184 to 186	Exercise 5.1 Points 1, 2 and 3	190
Copy, rename, and delete macros	Lesson 5.1 Titles 4 and 5	187 and 188	Exercise 5.1 Points 4 and 5	190
Create and modify form	Lesson 4.1 Titles 1, 2 and 6	148, 149 and 152	Exercise 4.1 Points 1, 2 and 6	154, and 155

TABLE OF OBJECTIVES

Tasks	Lessons	Pages	Exercises	Pages
Create and modify a form control (e.g., add an item to a drop-down list)	Lesson 4.1 Titles 3, 4 and 5	149 to 151	Exercise 4.1 Points 3, 4 and 5	155
Use advanced text alignment features with graphics	Lesson 1.4 Title 5	64	Exercise 1.4 Point 5	70
Customize toolbars	Lesson 5.2 Titles 1 and 2	194 and 197	Exercise 5.2 Points 1 and 2	199
Collaborating with workgroups				
Insert comments	Lesson 5.3, Title 1	202	Exercise 5.3 Point 1	218
Protect documents	Lesson 5.3 Titles 3 and 4	208 and 210	Exercise 5.3 Points 3 and 4	218
Create multiple versions of a document	Lesson 5.3 Titles 5 and 6	211	Exercise 5.3 Points 5 and 6	219
Track changes to a document	Lesson 5.3 Title 2	204	Exercise 5.3 Point 2	218
Set default file location for workgroup templates	Lesson 5.3 Title 7	214	Exercise 5.3 Point 7	219
Round Trip documents from HTML	Lesson 5.3 Title 8	216	Exercise 5.3 Point 8	219

A

AUTOTEXT

Changing 19
Creating 15
Deleting 19
Using 17

B

BOOKMARK

Create 115
Delete 116
Use 117

BORDER

For several paragraphs 74
On the first page 83

BREAK

Between lines and paragraphs 78
Inserting 75

C

CALCULATION

Addition 27
Calculation functions in a table 29
Formatting the result 30
Formulas in a table 28

CHART

Adding a title 55
Creating 48
Formatting 55
Leaving Microsoft Graph 50
Managing the legend 54
Series in rows/columns 53
Type 53
See also DATASHEET

CHECK BOX

See FORM

COLOUR

Paragraphs 74

COLUMN

Adding 27
Inserting a break 75
Sort 27
Width 76

INDEX

COMMENT

Create	202
Delete	203
Edit	203
Print	204
Viewing	203

See also VERSION

COPY

Excel data into Word by linking	36
Macro project	189

CROSS-REFERENCE

Create	117

D

DATA FILE

See MAIL MERGE

DATA FORM

See RECORD

DATASHEET

Clearing cells	49
Deleting rows/columns	49
Entering data	49
Importing an Excel worksheet	51

See also CHART

DELETE

AutoText	19
Bookmark	116
Comments	204
Macro	187
Macro project	189
Object	63
Record	170
Rows/columns in the datasheet	49
Style	96
Tool from a toolbar	195
Version	212

DIMENSIONS

See SIZE

DOCUMENT

Associating a password	210
Linking to a template	102
Protect	208

See also VERSION

DROP-DOWN LIST

See FORM

E

EMBED

Changing an embedded worksheet	39

Excel worksheet into
a Word document 32

ENDNOTE

See FOOTNOTE

F

FIELD

See FORM, MAIL MERGE

FIELD CODES

Showing/hiding 31

FIND

Formatting 13
Record (mail merge) 168
Special characters 14

FOLDER

Default workgroup templates
folder 214

FOOTER

On the first page 82

FOOTNOTES

Changing the appearance 113
Changing the numbering 114

Changing where the notes
are printed 113
Create 110
Using the notes pane 111

FORM

Check box properties 151
Create 148
Drop-Down list properties 150
Inserting form fields 149
Protect 152
Text field properties 149
Use 153

FORMAT

Chart 55
Finding/replacing 13

FRAME

See BORDER

H

HEADER

On the first page 82

HTML

See INTERNET EXPLORER

I

INDEX

Create 129
Defining an index entry 130
Inserting an index 132
Updating 132

INTERNET EXPLORER

Going from Word
to Internet Explorer 216
Retrieving an HTML page
in Word 215

L

LABEL

Create 171

LEVEL

Paragraph outline levels 125

LINE

Widow/orphan 78

LINK

See COPY, EMBED, TEMPLATE

LIST

Sort 24

M

MACRO

Create 184
Delete 187
Editing 186
Running 185
See also MACRO PROJECT

MACRO PROJECT

Copy 189
Delete 189
Rename 189
See also MACRO

MAIL MERGE

Associating a data file
to the main document 164
Creating a data file 161
Creating the main document 160
Inserting a field 164
Managing the records
in a data file 168
Merging according
to certain criteria 166
Merging only certain records 165
Running 165
Steps of creation 160

See also RECORD, LABEL

MASTER DOCUMENT

Create   140
Use   140

MERGING DOCUMENTS

See TRACKING CHANGES

MICROSOFT EXCEL

Changing an Excel worksheet
inserted in a Word document   38
Copying Excel data into Word
by linking   36
Embedding an Excel worksheet
into a Word document   32
Importing an Excel worksheet
into a chart   51

MICROSOFT GRAPH

See CHART

MOVE

Object   63
See also POSITION

N

NUMBERING

Footnotes   114

O

OBJECT

Deleting   63
Moving   63
Position   66
Sizing   63
Wrapping   64

ORPHAN

See LINE

OUTLINE

Creating a table of contents
from an outline   128
Creating an outline using
preset styles   124
Paragraph outline levels   125
Use   126

P

PAGE

Border   74
Particular layout for the first
Page   82
See also HEADER, BORDER

INDEX

PARAGRAPH

Fill colour   74
Managing line and
paragraph breaks   78
Outline level   125
Sort   12

PASSWORD

Associating with a document   210
See also PROTECTION

PICTURE

Inserting from a file   62

POSITION

Object   67
See also MOVE

PRINT

Comments   204
Footnotes   113
List of styles   97

PROTECTION

Document   208
Form   152
See also PASSWORD

R

RECORD

Accessing the data form   168
Add   168
Delete   170
Find   168
Modify   170
Sort   171

REPLACE

Formatting   13
Special characters   14

ROW

Adding   27

S

SIZE

Object   63

SORT

Date file   171
List   24
One column in a table   27
Paragraphs   12
Table   25

SPECIAL CHARACTERS

Finding/replacing   14

STYLE

Apply   93
Create   90
Delete   96
Display   98
Modify   95
Outline level   125
Print   97
See also OUTLINE

T

TABLE

Managing a table as
in a spreadsheet   28
Sort   25
*See also COLUMN, ROW,
CALCULATION*

TABLE OF CONTENTS

Create   128
Updating   129

TEMPLATE

Based on an existing document 100
Based on an existing template 99
Defining the default workgroup
templates folder   214
Linking to a document   102
Modify   101

TEXT FIELD

See FORM

TICK BOX

See FORM

TOOL

Add   195
Customising the appearance   196
Delete   195
See also TOOLBAR

TOOLBAR

Create   197
Customising   194

TRACKING CHANGES

Accepting or rejecting changes 206
Document available to several
users   204
Merging documents   206

U

UPDATE

Index   132
Table of contents   129

INDEX

USER

Document available to several
users   204
See also TRACKING CHANGES

V

VERSION

Create   211
Delete   212
Open   211
Viewing the comments   213

VIEW

Comments   203
Field codes   31

VISUAL BASIC

See MACRO

W

WATERMARK

Creating   81

WEB PAGE

See INTERNET EXPLORER

WIDOW

See LINE

WIDTH

Column   76

WORKSHEET

See MICROSOFT EXCEL

WRAP

Object   64

List of available titles in
the Microsoft Office User Specialist collection

Visit our Internet site for the list of the latest titles published.
http://www.eni-publishing.com

ACCESS 2000
EXCEL 2000 CORE
EXCEL 2000 EXPERT
EXCEL 2002 EXPERT
OUTLOOK 2000
POWERPOINT 2000
WORD 2000 CORE
WORD 2000 EXPERT
WORD 2002 EXPERT